"*But Your Mother Loves You* is a powerful story of love denied, loss, healing, restoration, and the resiliency of the human spirit when God is allowed in. It is masterfully told in a fresh and authentic voice. Riveting!"

— Karen Abercrombie, Award-winning Actress,
Singer, and Storyteller

"You will find this incredible story of redemption hard to believe, but you cannot make this stuff up, folks! I'll bet that you've never read one of God's love stories told in this manner–with so much sarcasm and unfiltered insults. To know Kim Honeycutt is to experience God's desperate, relentless, passionate pursuit for her. That she has written her story to share with the world speaks to how desperately God wants us to know His propensity for redemption the way she does."

— Dr. Lucretia Carter Berry, Co-Founder of Brownicity,
Educator, and Author of *What LIES Between Us*

"At the heart of every transformation, there is transparency. *But Your Mother Loves You* offers vulnerable yet practical principles that anyone can use and the story leaves the heart saying, "me too." Kim Honeycutt writes with the freedom that comes from facing your challenges head on and mastering your identity through Christ to help rid yourself of toxic love."

— Stephen Scoggins, Founder and CEO
of The Journey Principles Institute

"From the first few lines of the very first chapter, I felt as though Kim Honeycutt was speaking directly to me. This book felt relational from the very start. The humor, wit, and authenticity were refreshing. Kim Honeycutt has truly stepped out with a boldness and fearlessness evidenced by complete vulnerability in such a way that would provoke, challenge and encourage the very souls of her readers. To anyone who's ever had a hang up or hurt directly tied to ANY relationship, this book is totally for you. And, if you've ever wanted to experience healing from those relationships, this is a good place to start."

— Matthew Slyman, CEO and
Producer of CrossWorks Studio

But Your Mother Loves You

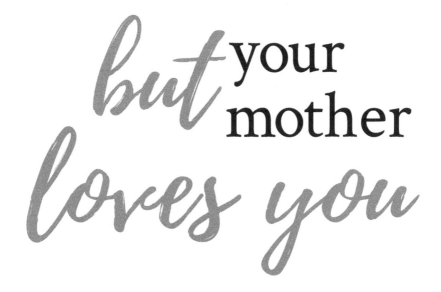

but your mother loves you

How to Overcome the Cycle of Toxic Love
and Live Your Life Without Shame

kim b. honeycutt
LCSW, LCAS

NEW YORK

LONDON • NASHVILLE • MELBOURNE • VANCOUVER

But Your Mother Loves You

How to Overcome the Cycle of Toxic Love and Live Your Life Without Shame

Published in New York, New York, by Morgan James Publishing. Morgan James is a trademark of Morgan James, LLC. www.MorganJamesPublishing.com

ISBN 9781642791914 paperback
ISBN 9781642791921 eBook
Library of Congress Control Number: 2018910662

Cover Design by:
Megan Dillon
megan@creativeninjadesigns.com

Interior Design by:
Chris Treccani
www.3dogcreative.net

Morgan James is a proud partner of Habitat for Humanity Peninsula and Greater Williamsburg. Partners in building since 2006.

Get involved today! Visit
MorganJamesPublishing.com/giving-back

To all those whose pain, trauma, and
life experiences have been invalidated,
please know *I see you*.
To all those who have supported the creation and
continuation of icuTalks ministry, thank you for
encouraging others and me to share our stories.

TABLE OF CONTENTS

FOREWORD

This is an interesting position in which to be—a place where I do not know if I am more proud or humbled to be writing the foreword for *But Your Mother Loves You*. I think this is because this is not just a book. It is the vulnerable life story of one of the most relentless people I know—Kim Honeycutt.

This book, Kim's life, will undoubtedly push you toward certain freedom. It will be a freedom from the fear of people—what they can do to you and their expectations of you. This freedom is not simply an optimistic hope, but it's an undeniable reality for Kim. She has fought hard to break free and to remain free.

In the pages of *But Your Mother Loves You*, Kim goes back into the "battle" for freedom in order to set others free. She has pronounced war against the enemies of the human soul. She is going after shame, insecurity, and negative self worth, and she takes no prisoners. This is why Kim is such an inspirational example for us all.

But Your Mother Loves You is real. It tells the story of harsh life situations and also offers realistic solutions. Written in Kim's down-to-earth and witty style, it is a book that does not run away from pain, grief, or ambiguity but rather runs towards them all. Make no mistake; this book will move you from mediocrity to audacity in your own pursuit of freedom.

She is convinced of the power within her, the One who empowers her to do more than she is capable of accomplishing on her own. This power is her anchor; it is her nourishment and her joy. This power is God's love, exemplified by Jesus's death on the cross and extended by the Holy Spirit now living in her.

But Your Mother Loves You is a dream come true. It's a vision fulfilled and a prayer answered. It is a testimony to God's faithfulness and Kim's tenacity. It stirs us to pursue our own goals and dreams, secure in the knowledge that God is with us.

Finally, this book is only the beginning. It is the beginning of Kim's impact on a larger community, for it will be the beginning of healing for so many. Today, it is the beginning of the work God wants to do for, in, and through you.

My prayer is that *But Your Mother Loves You* will bother you in a good way. I pray it motivates you to push past your own fears, offenses, and regrets and press into the healing and purpose God has for you. My final prayer is an echo of Kim's prayer: We are believing that you will not allow the enemy to kill, steal, or destroy your faith, love, and hope.

Enjoy...and get to work.

Naeem Fazal, Founding Pastor Mosaic Church and Author of *Ex-Muslim*

ACKNOWLEDGMENTS

First and foremost, I would like to acknowledge the Jesus that knew me and loved me, even when the only way His name would escape my mouth was to curse. He is now the Jesus to Whom I pray, and His Way is my saving grace. I praise the One whose pain gives purpose to mine and the Father whose Holy Spirit patiently transformed me from nothing to something, from rejected to accepted.

To my mother, I love you exactly as you are. It hurt me to write out our truth, but please know it hurt me more when I kept the pain inside. Because of our joint courage, others will be set free. I pray you never again believe the lies that entangled both of us for decades. For freedom, we have been set free.

To my daddy, your bright shades of love cannot be measured, dulled, or contained. Thank you for showing me what grace and mercy look like on this earth. If I ever find a man like you, I will get married. I can say with confidence your exemplary character cannot be duplicated; therefore, I am guaranteed a single life. You are my favorite person. I love you, Daddy!!!

I would like to give a ginormous shout out to my BFF, Danski, who is a walking ministry. Because of your friendship, I have been adopted into a secure and normal family (so weird to consider one exists, but apparently it does). Somehow, even when my self-hatred was raging, you could only see Christ within me. I am saddened when I think there are people who may never meet you. For, to know you is to be encouraged and to know Him.

Dearest Cortney, you are my ghostwriter (if y'all find mistakes, it is on her and not me), editor, partner in ministry, but most important of all, friend in Christ. Without you, a story that has the potential to help so many, would have remained trapped in my busy schedule, fears, and voice-infested head. Thank you for being exactly who you are.

I would like to thank my pastor, Naeem Fazal, and his wife, Ashley Fazal. You have both encouraged me to get uncomfortable in my faith and helped me create a bridge so that I could walk onto a beautiful platform to share about God's redeeming love. Naeem, I would have never had the courage to audition to be a TEDx speaker without your influence. You are a safe man in my life, and you will never know how healing that is for me. Ashley, you are the friend who can gently support me while simultaneously kicking me in the rear end when I am experiencing paralysis. Thank you for getting me. Thank you both for creating a Mosaic community where people belong before they believe.

To all of my Mosaic Charlotte church family, I thank you for being patient and loving as God molded me into the speaker I am today.

I would also like to thank Linda Currie, Christine Zazzaro, John Lee, Ruthie Epting, Connie Burns, Vijay Director, and Ann Siegel for being safe mental health professionals who taught me to get out of my head and find safety in my body, which led to my spiritual and emotional restoration.

To every person who walked the walk with me in the rooms of Alcoholics Anonymous, I thank you. You taught me things I never would have learned elsewhere. You are the first group of people who taught me the value of "me too."

I would be remiss if I didn't thank the many clients/patients who walk into my psychotherapy office and sit face to face with me, the ones who share their fears, shame, and horrific trauma. While the therapeutic relationship is primarily about you, I have grown with you.

I want to thank the Columbia College staff, faculty, and all my c'sters. I wouldn't be where I am today if God had not sent me to a school with people who refused to be bystanders to my self-destruction. I particularly want to acknowledge the late Mitzi Winesett for being my wounded healer.

To the Fort Mill High School class of '89, thank you all for still being in my life and accepting me when I found myself unacceptable.

Morgan James Publishing, thank you for accepting my truth and affirming my belief that I have something significant to share. Tiffany Gibson, Author Relations Manager extraordinaire, I appreciate your excitement and swift answers to my questions along the way.

A huge thank you to everyone who has ever attended an icuTalks event! To the volunteers and speakers, you have created an atmosphere for people to know their struggles are real and allow them to be real in the struggle.

Finally, to my Uncle Joe who is now with Jesus, I thank you so much for being my favorite uncle. Thank you for riding with my dad to the hospital to be by my side. You have always been right beside me. I love and miss you tremendously.

CHAPTER 1
MY STORY

We are ashamed to tell our story
when we believe shame is our story.

~ KBH

t's the end of my first month at college. It has been roughly thirty days living out from under the roof that houses the stress and pain caused by the dysfunctional relationship I have with my mother. There has been a wonderful taste of freedom! And, taste I have. Budweiser. Rolling Rock. Michelob Light. I am making friends and attending classes. Life seems pretty good, and I feel relaxed, perhaps for the first time in a long time.

I feel a measure of acceptance. The staff and students at Columbia College are exceptional. I have a sense of contentment, too. It's something I am not used to. Perhaps it's stemming from more free time to drink. Regardless, it's delightfully different.

I think to myself that it is time to reconnect. It's time to check in with my family. After all, I do miss my daddy. So, I take the initiative and pick up the phone.

My mother answers on the second ring. I will never forget the straightforward and harsh words she speaks when I say *hi, Mom*.

"You don't need to call here. No one here wants to talk to you."

I slowly hang up; her words reverberate in my mind, echo in my soul. I immediately feel rejected. Shocked. Sad. These feelings are nothing new.

So, I reach for another bottle, and I feel nothing more.

Conversation with My Mother:

Mother: "They finally wrote a book about how to be a parent. I want to get it and read it."

Kim: "Why Mother? It's a little late; don't you think?"

Mother: "I just want to see how many mistakes I made."

Kim: "Mother, there isn't a big enough book for that."

Mother: "You are so encouraging."

Kim: "Yeah."

Mother: "Well, I heard that the book says parents aren't supposed to solve their children's problems. They are supposed to let them figure them out so they can grow up."

Kim: "I have been teaching parents that for years, Mom."

Mother: "Did your father and I do that for you?"

Kim: "You definitely did not solve my problems. You left me to my own devices (vices, really)."

Mother: "You mean like telling you when you were in college not to call home?"

Kim: "Yes, Mother. Exactly."

These days, I am highly entertained by my conversations with my mother, particularly this one. She thought the first parenting book was published in 2015, a full four decades after my birth!

We all have a mother.

It's just the way it is. Some mothers are delightful people who create safe environments for their children to grow. Other mothers are distant, perhaps to the point of neglectfulness. Some are powerful or determined. Others are timid or take a back seat within the family dynamics. There are mothers who work full time and ones who stay home (which is full time work as well). Mothers are as varied in personalities, strengths, and even dysfunctional characteristics as they are numerous. There is, however, one trait all mothers share. They are all influential. For better or for worse, our mothers impact us deeply.

It's a southern-style steamy summer morning as I back out of my garage. I live forty-five minutes away from my parents. It's close enough – close enough in proximity to attend holiday gatherings without inconvenience but far enough away that my mother can say she can't come see me because of the distance. As I exit my garage, my iPhone (his name is Troy, by the way) buzzes, and the screen on my car displays "mother."

Normally, I would assume something is wrong since she rarely calls me. However, on this particular day, I am able to make a safe assumption as to why "mother" is illuminated on my screen. There is no emergency. I push the receive button and my guess is confirmed. I instantly hear my mother singing "Happy Birthday" in her Americanized-but-still-accented tone. I wait for her to finish singing.

Finally, she says, "Happy Birthday, Daughter!"

"Thank you, Mother," I respond. "But today is the eleventh."

My mother emphatically states, "Yes, and this is your day of birth."

"Actually, Mom, my birthday is the twelfth. I was born on the twelfth. My birthday is tomorrow."

"Well, this is close enough."
"Yes, Mother. It's close enough."

I didn't grow up knowing or experiencing the love of my mother. In fact, our relationship was what I later learned to label as "toxic." I never felt good enough. My mother is crazy. Having a crazy mom is very different than having a mom who is crazy in love with you. I truly am grateful that so many people have moms that are nurturing and crazy in love with them. That is not my experience. When I say I have a crazy mother, I mean she struggles emotionally and mentally. Do I believe that most of us do? Of course I do. I am a psychotherapist, and I know that we all struggle emotionally and mentally to various degrees. My mother did the best she could, and at some point during my emotional and mental struggles, I had to decide that her best wasn't mine.

This leads us to my huge SPOILER ALERT! As no surprise to those who know me, I have done this thing backwards. This is the conclusion to my story, the climactic ending of a decades-long journey.

My mother and I now have a good relationship! Let me be clear: We have a good relationship *today*. Today, it holds respect, boundaries, and humor. Today, I am able to tell you that we are friends. I could not have said that for the majority of my life. I've given away the ending of this book in order to track backwards and explain the *how*.

How did my mother and I get here? How did we reach a place of mutuality—a place where she and I have found friendship—especially given the trauma, pain, and choices of my childhood and adolescence that I have shared in the following chapters? It wasn't easy. You could say it all started with a thousand paper cuts and a few crucial phone calls.

Whenever my mother calls me, I smile in anticipation and pick up Troy (my iPhone, people!). Mostly humorous, our conversations are a connection—a dialog that's as unique as our relationship. Throughout the book, I include some of these chats not to poke fun at my mother, but to offer a further peek into my life. I realize that our expression of love and how we communicate with each other may seem bizarre to you. It isn't bizarre for us. For us, it is authentic connection, connection that was mended after having been broken by trauma.

Successful relationships rarely look the way we think they will, and they are almost never as fluid as presented in the media. My mother and I fought incessantly—until I learned to surrender my expectations and release my disappointments. She would yell. I would freeze in my tracks and stare at her. When we encounter trauma in a relationship, we freeze, fight, or flee. Most of the time, I froze but an internal battle would ensue. I wasn't the daughter she wanted, and I realized she wasn't the mother I wanted or needed. Once I understood that I did not have to change to meet her ideal nor did she have to change to meet mine, our healing started to occur.

This does not mean that I didn't change. It means I stopped waiting for her to change—specifically to like me. At one point, I took some time and stepped away from our relationship. (To make it sound nice, let's call it a sabbatical). During this break, I stopped focusing on the thought that she didn't like me, and I hyper-focused on the fact that I didn't like myself. At this point, I knew that God sent His Son for me. If I had been the only one on this earth, He would have still sent His Son just for me. Once I absorbed this spiritual nugget of pure truth, I knew I had no right to not like myself. I took the time that was necessary to eradicate the self-hatred and to put His love in those deep places (John 3:30).

All of us have a responsibility to bring death to the lies of this world, the ones that reside within us. Many of my shame-drenched lies came from my mother. No matter who tries to tether us to the incredibly limited beliefs of this world, it is our responsibility to bring truth to those areas. I knew if I was to be renewed I had to face my deepest pain without believing I was the pain. I couldn't do this and continue to interact with my mother. I took a break from our relationship, which was easy because she didn't want me around anyway.

Part of the purpose of this book is to challenge you, my reader friends, to remember that my mother isn't your mother. People tend to hear half of a story about my mother or a tiny portion about my childhood and interrupt me and make the claim, "But your mother loves you." I find this happens often on the social media giant, Facebook, too. "But your mother loves you" snakes its way into the comments section of many of my posts. Those who give voice to the claim "But your mother loves you" are 1) basing their statement on their own nurturing and emotionally present mother 2) speaking from a place of avoiding conflict in their own mother-daughter relationship, or 3) speaking out of guilt or shame from the way they parented their own children.

This is the crux of my story. Well, this and the fact that God pursues us even when we don't know Him. God is relentlessly weaving us back into the stories He wrote for us when He created us, even as we run the other way, penning our own self-destructive adventures.

We all have a story. I have met thousands of people over the years. I've built most of my adult life around sharing my story and listening to others share theirs as I provide therapy to help them navigate the challenges of their own difficult tales. God asked me to restore my relationship with my mother by trusting Him. Now I am being asked to really, really trust Him by risking the very relationship

I have worked to reconcile by writing my story. I don't know exactly what the consequences will be for telling my story. I do know there will be less consequences than if I didn't tell it at all. I believe we keep our stories buried deep within our own self-made tombs when we don't realize we are worthy of being resurrected. I believed the lies of the world for many years as evidenced by alcoholism, self-mutilation, eating disorders, and other behaviors that dripped with self-hatred.

My story—just like yours—is worth telling. So many of us have felt (or still feel) not good enough. That is one of the lies of our enemy. I know this to be true: Our stories matter. They highlight the unchanging love of our God. They give Him the glory. They are *worth telling.*

This tale is about how God used my mother's and my chaotic, dysfunctional, and evolving relationship to showcase His redeeming love and grace. It's a story I feel compelled to tell in order to help others find grace and peace, despite their toxic relationships. I want others to know they are truly good enough. My story may not be special, but it is authentic: authentically flawed, authentically humorous, and authentically vulnerable.

No one benefits from being perfect. As a matter of fact, participation in perfectionism is acting out in an addiction. We cannot be who we are called to be if we are shielding our shame and blame with perfectionism. Perfectionism is born from shame. We were born from God's conception and called to live in His image. Shame calls us to hide who we are in a worldly image. We are more than that. We are more than good enough. I am authentically *imperfect*. Thanks to my mother, I am really, really good at being authentically imperfect. I believe authentically driven people neither avoid looking at their past nor do they stare in the rearview mirror. They have looked at it thoroughly enough that it is no longer the driver of their life, nor the unexpected bump in the road. If authentic imperfection resonates with you, then keep reading. I hope you enjoy this testimony about my mother, our struggle, and me.

CHAPTER 2

MOTHER

Stop believing you are the reflection of
someone else's deflection.

~ KBH

My relationship with my mother is messy. If you met her, you would not see anything messy or disorganized about her. She is beautifully "put together," from her impeccably styled hair to her sophisticated designer clothes. She is the type of individual who goes to high-class restaurants that boast two-hour waits. She isn't one to wait, however. The owners of these restaurants notice my mother instantly, and they proceed to personally escort her past all who are waiting and gracefully deliver her to the best table. Something similar happens with high-end clothing stores as well. Fashion empires like Neiman Marcus, St. John, and Burberry actually call my mother to let her know when they've received new items she might like.

Mother is a speedster! I wholeheartedly admit this is one characteristic I inherited from her. There was one extraordinary day, back in my youth, when she was pulled over twice for two different traffic violations—within hours of each other! Neither officer gave her a ticket. Yep, my mother makes (and leaves) quite an impression.

Even her name is fancy: Xenia Del Carmen Bandini. She is from Panama and immigrated to the United States when she was nine years old. She, her mother, and her four siblings left everything they had and everyone they knew in order to escape troubling circumstances in Panama.

There were many changes all at once. When my mother came to America, she left almost everything familiar behind, including her father. She also left behind a bright red bike with her name on it. She loved that bike; it was one of a few material items that her siblings could never confuse as their own.

Even integrating into the school system was difficult. The education system would not let her attend school until she learned English. Therefore, my mother sat in front of a television for months—not as a means of escape or for entertainment, but to learn English and be able to seek academic fulfillment. Her transition to the English language was anything but fluid, and as a result, she never taught me her native tongue. I was well into adulthood before I realized the resiliency she must have possessed in order to accomplish all she had as a little girl.

Xenia is a physically beautiful woman—a Latina with dark hair, dark eyes, and dark skin. She believes posture and poise are crucial to maintaining a respectable appearance. My mother was "one of those mothers" who tried to get me to walk around with a book on my head.

She does not look her age and likely never will. One day about five years ago, my mother went to the doctor. On the intake forms, she wrote down her birthday. When the staff processed her paperwork, they couldn't believe her age.

Mother is fiery, too. She can cuss me out in Spanish for two solid minutes without blinking, or perhaps even breathing. When I was growing up, she would throw things when she became upset. My mother was the type of woman who could be screaming and hurling things one minute, and then the phone would ring (back in the day when the phone was attached to a wall). Her tone and entire demeanor would do a 180-degree turn, and she would answer in the most calm and composed tone: *Hello*. While this seems to be a common and humorous scenario that standup comedians use in their bits, as a psychotherapist, I happen to know this behavior can contribute to a disorganized attachment in children.

My mother spent a lot of time dieting, which had a profound impact on me. In fact, the negative consequences of watching her obsess about weight have spanned my entire life. Her outward appearance is paramount to how she feels on the inside. That vain spirit filters down into all her relationships, too. My mother is judgmental and has extremely high standards. She lacks the ability to communicate with compassion. These are some of the many ways we are different.

Conversation with My Mother:

Kim: "How did it go, Mother?"

Mother: "It went well. I met a woman who just returned from Germany."

Kim: "You graduated from high school in Germany, didn't you Mom?"

Mother: "Yes, so we talked about Germany, and she showed me pictures. Then the woman said I should return to Germany with my daughter."

Kim: "What did you say to that?"

> Mother: "I told her you don't know my daughter. She won't go anywhere. She is a workaholic. She is just like her father!"
> Kim: "Awwww, Mom, that is the nicest thing you have ever said to me. I love being compared to dad!"

One Father's Day celebration not too long ago, my entire family met at the luxurious Ballantyne Resort in Charlotte, North Carolina. If you're unfamiliar with it, think Ritz Carlton Hotel but with the addition of golf courses and a spa. We were having a meal at the lavish restaurant, and my mother was horrified to receive a "to-go" bag from the server. Worse than simply receiving it, my mother was appalled that the server had placed it on the empty chair next to her.

"Seats are made for sitting, not for doggie bags," she reprimanded the poor young woman who was simply trying to attend to her customer. Not many people can do right in the eyes of my mother.

My mother favors being alone, yet I imagine she also feels alone. There are often times when she is convinced everyone hates her. She makes every effort to avoid overtly public places such as hospitals, sporting events, and graduation ceremonies. She prefers immediate family or small gatherings in the comfort of her home or a nice restaurant. While I was young, she did have two parties at our house. I'll get into the significance of those soon. She frequently gardened. It was a quiet hobby in the privacy of her yard.

Conversation with My Mother:
Kim: "Good morning, Mother!"
Mother: "Who are you talking to?"
Kim: "You, Mother."
Mother: "Who is in the car with you?"
Kim: "No one, Mother. I'm on my way to the office."

Mother: "Ok, then I will talk to you."

My mother struggles with paranoia and agoraphobia, the extreme or irrational fear of crowded spaces or enclosed public places. It started with seemingly mild symptoms. My mother would conceal herself in quiet parts of the house when I was a child. To this day, she still only pops out into the community for a few moments to eat brunch with the family about three times per year or to go clothes shopping. After awhile, she runs away to the comfort of her car until whomever she is with is ready to go home. Her insecurity demands isolation. She avoids small talk as best she can.

Xenia took her first trip back to Panama since immigrating to the States when I was in the third grade. It proved to trigger too much pain for her. While the onset of PTSD (Post-Traumatic Stress Disorder) occurred in her childhood, this trip resulted in a reemergence of her symptoms.

She was never the same. Her agoraphobia worsened tremendously. For example, Mother would pull into the Springs Complex in Fort Mill, South Carolina in her green 280z and drop me off at the ball field. No worries: There will be more on my heroic baseball career later. Then, she would listen to the voice of shame and park nearby and wait for me. The fact that she didn't watch my games—even though almost every other child had a parent who was present—never consciously bothered me. She delivered me to the practices and games, which seemed like enough at the time. Despite her mental illness, Mother did often go to my school to deal with "issues" that arose with my behavior or choices. After all, she was protective of our family's reputation.

My mother and my daddy (yes, I use formal and informal designations respectively) met while he was in college, and within a suitable time frame, they married. It had been a blind date that solidified my future existence. At first, my mother was concerned that she was dating a man from the small and "unknown" town of Fort Mill, South Carolina. However, my daddy wooed her with his personable demeanor, extraordinary intellect, and unparalleled patience.

You see, my mother understands that intelligence is vital to survival and certainly significant to maintaining an elevated socio-economic level in the community. She had taught herself English when she arrived in America by watching television. As a Hispanic girl in New York City in the 1950's, there was little emphasis put on her formal education, and that stung. I imagine it caused her feelings of inadequacy and inferiority. She married my daddy despite her reservations about his hometown. And, he married her, not realizing there was deep-rooted psychological wounding living below the surface of her elitism and vanity.

Six years into their marriage, my mother became pregnant. She was raised Catholic, so she did what came natural to her. She prayed fervently to our Heavenly Father for a blonde-haired, blue-eyed, light-skinned "American" baby. She had grown up within the limitations of blatant discrimination. In her own way, she loved her unborn baby enough to realize she wanted life to be different for her child. Her prayers were answered, but it was with a resounding, "No!"

My brother entered this world with my mother's olive complexion, dark brown hair, and piercing dark eyes. In my family, we call this appearance "brack" —a mixture of brown and black eyes. It didn't take long for my mother to fall in love with her "brack-eyed" baby who looked just like her. Have you ever noticed how mothers have significant attachments with their sons, particularly if they are the first-born? I think this phenomenon crosses all cultures but seems particularly true in the Hispanic community.

Excited about her first-born child, she named him Golden Boy. Okay, that isn't his real name, but it might as well be. She showed him off like a prized trophy. She still does. My friends and I refer to him as Jimmy Jimmy Jimmy because when my mother speaks of him she becomes excited and says his name numerous times.

Conversation with My Mother:

Mother: "Jimmy Jimmy Jimmy. I love Jimmy. Jimmy is the best thing I ever did. Jimmy Jimmy Jimmy's birthday is in a few days. Jimmy Jimmy Jimmy. What should I get Jimmy for his birthday?"

Kim: (involuntary scream) "I don't care what you get him!"

Mother: "Now, Kim."

Kim: "Just get him something expensive."

Mother: "Ok. Well... I'm gonna let you go. Have a wonderful day and keep society going for us."

Really? I don't know what that means, but I am sure it has something to do with my brother's birthday!

I am not saying my brother was somehow protected or that he was unscathed from my mother's illness. However, his story isn't my story to tell. In my non-humble opinion, she over attached to him but was still an inconsistent parent. This is called ambivalent attachment. I don't know my brother very well. We had very different childhoods. I do know he loves the Lord, and that is wonderful news.

Eight months after my brother entered the world, I was conceived, though it's best for me to believe a turkey baster was involved. My mother instantly started to pray again. She prayed for a child like Jimmy Jimmy Jimmy, (I mean Golden Boy...I mean just Jimmy) one with dark skin, brown eyes, and dark hair.

The Honeycutt family of three would soon become a family of three plus one.

CHAPTER 3

ME

If someone is mistreating you,
make sure you aren't treating yourself
in the same manner.

~ KBH

Hi. My name is Kim. I'm an alcoholic. Actually, I'm a recovered alcoholic. Officially, I am Kim Berly Honeycutt. I am the one who severed my first name (Kimberly) to create a unique middle name (Berly) just to harass my parents. After all, the middle name they chose for me was horrendous. No, that's not completely true. It's just not congruent with my personality. It is a "nice person's" name and those who know me, know that I don't need a nice person's name. I am not going to tell you what the name is; undoubtedly, one of you reading this has been "blessed" with the name. And, Yvette, I don't want you to put the book down quite yet. ☺

My dad was in the military when I was born. After law school, he was drafted and became an attorney in the Vietnam War. So, I entered this world at Ireland Army Community Hospital in Fort

Knox, Kentucky. It's interesting to note that they are only open from 9:00 a.m. to 5:00 p.m.

I was not surprised to learn I was a breech baby. There were no extra measures to remedy that situation, and out I came. I like to think I was born feet first so I could run. There is literal and figurative meaning in this statement. I lost some oxygen in the process of my birth. I wish this fact explained everything. That, however, would make for a very short book.

I cost my parents only $7.50, which was the total hospital bill for my delivery. Unfortunately, that did little to comfort my mother who had prayed for a "brack-eyed" baby and bore me instead. I felt like Steve Martin in the movie, *The Jerk*. He was the white child born into a brown family. Maybe that is why I have always loved Steve Martin. (Side note: The last time I participated in Halloween was in the Fourth Grade, and I went as Steve Martin with an arrow through my head and everything. It was very realistic.) My fair skin, blonde hair, and blue eyes soon turned to fair skin, red hair, and brown eyes. Immediately, my appearance became one of several barriers between my mother and me.

As a child, I believed (and still do a little bit even today) that I would never be attractive because that adjective was a luxury reserved only for darker-skinned people. I have always been more attracted to those who have darker skin. Can you blame me? (Shemar Moore, if you are reading this, please contact me.)

Jimmy and I were opposites in every way. He was a musician from birth. I can't even sing off-key. I am pretty sure Mother had him via C-section for two reasons: 1) so he would look better from the get-go and 2) because he came out playing the drums, and she wanted to make room for all that action. Jimmy is a phenomenal drummer. I have always respected him for his passion and his artistic craft.

Music was not my area of expertise. I loved T-ball. My nickname in T-ball – and later softball – was Little Hank Aaron. If you don't know who that is then bless you. Just know Mr. Hank was brown. I preferred the mud, sweat, and grit of sports. My mother was appalled. Let's just say I would spit the mud out of my mouth so I could tell her that I just wanted to feel her

This is why I drank.

approval, but all my eccentric and classy mother could do was work diligently to ensure the mud didn't touch her hair.

The best way I can explain our relationship is from the viewpoint of a child. Visualize a little girl running toward her mother with her hands raised up. Just before she gets to her mother, the little girl stops, turns to the side, and walks with her head and arms down. I wanted my mother to comfort me; however, she was the one who was hurting me, so I didn't know how to seek comfort from the one who was causing the pain. For most of my restorative relationship with her as an adult, I only raised my hands to God. As a result of that intimacy with God, one day I was able to raise my arms to my mother again. Through Him, I needed no dependence on her to reciprocate.

Conversation with My Mother:

Kim: "Hello, Mother. Please pray for me. I have to do what is called a peer to-peer review with an insurance company this morning. It means I have to talk to a doctor and convince him that my patient (whom I love) needs more therapy sessions."

Mother: "Well I will pray that you are brilliant. No, no. That is the wrong word."

Kim: "No, it isn't mom. You can say I am brilliant."

Mother: "No, I can't. It will cause you to have an EGO."

Kim: "Just say it. Say I am brilliant!"

Mother: "Your mom and dad think you are brilliant."

Kim: "NOOOO! Mother, you dissociated. It doesn't count if you say it in third person. People do that to separate from the sentiment." (FYI – part of having a disorganized attachment is dissociating through pronouns.)

Mother: "You are brilliant. We love you."

Kim: "I will take it!"

Because school and learning were so important to my parents, our childhood toys included electronic encyclopedias and other learning apparatuses. Ironically, I believe my mother harbors some level of envy about my academic successes (and of course, my sense of humor). She had her hand in the former and my dad, the latter. I think it is important to note my mother was the one who taught my brother and I to read at young ages. She was the one who purchased all the educational toys. Yes, my mother was the one who sat on the floor and reinforced all the information.

Sharing this part of my upbringing reminds me about a circumstance I encountered about five years ago. I was waiting semi-patiently at a small pharmacy while two moms with fifty-two kids in tow (okay, there were five, but it might as well have been fifty-two) were discussing how to educate their children. One mom divulged to the other one, "Did you know you don't have to read to your children? They learn how to read by talking to each other."

"Is that right?" replied mom #2, unquestioningly.

Because I know this isn't correct, I got back in my car with my Ritalin in my hand and called my mother. I let her know how appreciative I was about her intentionally educating me at home long before I entered the Fort Mill School System. I believe she championed my brother's and my education because of the rejection she experienced with her childhood school system. In this area of my life, she did for me what wasn't done for her. I will always be grateful. I would have never been able to appreciate this beautiful determination of hers if I had continued to minimize how she had victimized me in so many other ways. The clarity that comes from grace and mercy resides in the middle.

My family moved to Fort Mill, South Carolina when I was three. Somehow my dad convinced Xenia to return to his hometown to continue their family life together. To this day, she says, "Fort Millllllll" (long, drawn-out "l") If you hear her say it this way, you may think what I used to think—she is being condescending or that her high-class lips just cannot say it correctly. The truth is, it's the same reason she fires every pool company, landscaper, and other service-oriented professional. She dissociates and disconnects from certain people and places, no matter whom they are or if she has resided there for forty-four years. It doesn't matter that we are talking about Fort Mill; it could be anywhere. It's a coping strategy.

Fort Mill is a suburban town in York County, and it is the cutest town ever. It lies on the outskirts of Charlotte, North Carolina and is located north of the sprawling city of Rock Hill, or Rock Hillllllll. Her disconnection to these places is her acting just like me as a little girl in my previous example. Perhaps you have done it too? We run full sprint, hands outstretched towards something endearing and then at the last minute, we pull our hands down and run to the side to avoid any potential rejection. Sometimes, it is the best we can do.

My dad, James R. Honeycutt, immediately opened a private law practice. The fact that he was the only attorney in Fort Mill for a short while helped to convince my mother she would survive living there. Like the character "Norm" on the old sitcom *Cheers*, my dad was part of the fabric of Fort Mill where everybody knew his name. His personable and patient demeanor attracted everyone. Friends, neighbors, and other townspeople would stop by Jim's house for legal advice. He always gave it—usually at no cost.

He was (and is!) a good dad, too. When I was young, he showed me love, asked me if I was okay when I clearly I was not, looked me in the eyes with compassion, and was not embarrassed by me. He even called me cute. He cried at appropriate—albeit rare —times, and his tears left an incredible impression on me. I felt loved when he cried about things that mattered to me. I became a daddy's girl. I'm still a daddy's girl. One of my favorite things to do—both as a child and presently—is sit outside my parents' house on the front steps with him and talk. These moments incite my mother. They are when I feel the closest to him, and somehow the connection we have is a threat to her. She is convinced we are plotting to kill her. It's yet another expression of her mental illness. I promise y'all; I wouldn't do well in prison, so she is safe!

Our neighborhood was established and quaint. No house looked the same, and there were no sidewalks. The dozens of kids who lived there rode their wheeled toys all through the streets. The downtown area was about a mile-and-a-half away, and I would walk to the dime store to steal (um, I mean buy) candy.

Our house at 105 West Gregg Street had a fenced backyard with a tree house, and the tree house even had a slide! My brother and I grew up with everything we needed and more. There were birthday parties in the yard with clowns and loads of presents. My daddy bought me any toy I wanted, including a go-kart for one ridiculously special year. At age seven, he gave me a pet bird. I named it "Digger Beer." I am fairly certain this was foreshadowing overlooked by the adults in my life. Over the years, he also gifted me with a moped for Christmas, a horse, and six cars.

We were, perhaps by most standards, spoiled, but it wasn't important to my brother or me to have all this stuff. We just did. My dad had grown up very poor, and he didn't want his kids to ever feel what he felt living in that condition. Jimmy Jimmy Jimmy and I still feel like material things make us more comfortable, but we don't attach them to our identities. Somehow through it all, we both learned to place our priorities on relationships. Now, that being said, there are a few people I would break up with if I were forced to choose between them or my Lexus. Just sayin'.

My Uncle Joe (Daddy's brother) lived on a street diagonally behind ours. I could run there in two minutes flat. My grandmother lived across from him. It seemed to be the picturesque small-town atmosphere. Yet, we all know how looks can be deceiving.

When I was in the first and second grades, I had an imaginary friend. His name was Charlie. Charlie was adorable. He had dark brown hair that was cut exactly like the motorcycle cop, Jon, on the show, *CHIPS*. Remember him? He was the blonde one. Charlie was my height and also my age, which would have been between eight and nine years old. He had very defined muscles, and on certain days, he had a pack of cigarettes rolled up in his right shirtsleeve.

Charlie loved Star Wars

Make no mistake, though. Charlie was a good influence. He loved to study, and he did well in school.

Charlie wore a plain, white t-shirt every day. It never had writing on it. My mother didn't allow us to wear t-shirts with writing, so I guess the same rule applied to my buddy, Charlie.

During this time in my life, if you saw me, you saw Charlie (well not really, but you know what I mean). He was my protector. We were always together, and his primary job was to keep the bad people away from me. He shielded me from the insults, the repeat rejections, and the hurling hurts. I'll expand on those later.

Yes, we were always together; we spent a lot of time playing in the front yard. So of course, when I trekked the half-mile from my house on Gregg Street to my paternal grandmother's house, Charlie was right there beside me.

One day while visiting my grandmother, who was a God-fearing and God-loving woman (the epitome of The Beatitudes), she inquired about him. It was a bright, sunny Saturday—the kind of weather that people in Seattle envy. Leaning over, inching her gentle face to directly in front of mine, she asked, "And, where is Charlie today?"

I looked her right in the eyes. "He killed himself," I replied, matter-of-factly. "He jumped off the Catawba River Bridge." He did not leave a note.

You would think that a sweet grandmother would be shocked to hear such outlandish commentary from her young grandchild. However, my grandmother was very familiar with unpredictable behavior. She had married a Honeycutt and by that point, she understood our gene pool; we were interesting, to say the least.

Please know this: I do not take suicide lightly. Charlie and his death were a reflection of my pain. I was not comfortable in my own skin. I felt like an outsider in my own family. Except for my Daddy who was able to connect with me by simply sitting beside me, no one else seemed to have any affection or approval for the redheaded, pale child who liked to play in the mud and whose imaginary friend cut his fictional life short.

I now know that others loved and adored me, but I was so consumed by my mother's rejection that I couldn't integrate their love into the deepest regions of my soul. In time, God would show me that while I was staring at my mother in disbelief and distrust, I couldn't see that on the periphery of my life were many loved ones trying to reach me. This is a significant reason why I encourage my patients today to do the work to discover their hurts and recognize new perspectives. For then, they can experience the very people, internal resources, and strategies they don't realize are present and keeping them going.

CHAPTER 4
PRETTY

God's plan for you is bigger than the labels placed on you.

~ KBH

A WORD FROM KIM'S GHOSTWRITER
I think it is important to take a short side step from Kim's narrative to insert my perspective as I attempt to co-write her story. This next chapter took months to draft, write, and edit. There were many times when Kim struggled to simply read through it. She is one of the most vulnerable people I know. However, vulnerability doesn't negate emotion. The pain that Kim experienced, and now must relive in order to share the redemption with you, is great. The memories these stories elicit are much like flashbacks experienced by warriors from their days in battle. While Kim is strong and emotionally well by all accounts, she is still human. We hope and pray her pain is not lost on you, the reader, despite her ability and desire to be transparent (and witty!). No one should diminish anyone's

pain in that way. In fact, we shouldn't moderate our own hurts in an effort to be "strong." God's strength is made perfect in our weakness (and pain). Our painful experiences may be in the past, healed, and scarred over. But, they are scars that can be reopened. God doesn't erase our scars. That would detract from the messages He wants us to share. It would minimize the connections we can make by telling our stories. Thank you for allowing Kim to be vulnerable and still hurt - thankfully in a healed and worthwhile way. Praise God!

What becomes of a nine-year-old girl who arranges for her imaginary friend to commit suicide? Nothing good—at least for a long while.

There are countless reasons for Charlie's shocking and sad demise. I could easily write it off with the fact that we live in a broken world. However, it's abundantly more than that. One of the main stimuli that profoundly influenced me and paved the way for this story is toxic love. This sounds like an oxymoron, doesn't it? It is the paradox of all paradoxes! Toxic love demands you to spend more time focused on being who you think your loved one wants you to be while they hyper-focus on your perceived flaws and deflect all personal reflection. Thankfully, my journey ultimately led me to find love inside the toxicity. Let's take a peek into my life before this particular event.

During the ages from birth through five years, every child experiences rapid growth physically, intellectually, and emotionally. This swift development prepares kids for the school-age stage when they will be interacting with countless other individuals outside of the family unit, learning new ideas, engaging in experimentation, and figuring out who they are and where they fit into this world. However, if between birth and five, there is anything besides secure attachment and health, (such as unhealthy attachment, no attachment, no nutrition from which to gain health, or no appropriate direction and guidance from caring parents or guardians) children become stunted relationally, physically, and emotionally.

I share all this because before age six, I was already getting cues from my mother and others about how I didn't belong. I had healthy meals most of the time, but my mother was strangely selective about what kind of food was allowed in the house. For example, if Dad brought home Bojangles (a Southern fast food restaurant known for its use of salt), he couldn't bring it inside. We had to sit on the balcony to eat.

I knew my daddy loved me, but I had no idea how to relate to my mother. I did not understand mental illness. No one discussed it with me. It was likely no one knew what was happening, much less could explain it. I was certain she didn't like me, and I rarely felt her love for me. In fact, most of the time, I felt I wasn't good enough for her love. There was very little attachment. I missed out on a critical area of development at the stage when we all need it most.

Attachment Theory was founded based on the joint work of British psychiatrist, John Bowlby, and Canadian developmental psychologist, Mary Ainsworth. They designed and tested secure, avoidant, and anxious attachment. American psychologist, Mary Main, was the researcher who identified and named disorganized attachment. Professionals in the field of psychology describe attachment as a "lasting psychological connectedness between human beings."

Mental health professionals like myself teach about the four attachment styles. It's a fancy way to say there are four ways we can bond or relate to others. One is healthy. The others are not, but they are definitely not a death sentence for your relationships either. In fact, only a small percentage of people have a secure attachment, and most people who live with the other three insecure attachments can do well in relationships. These four styles are called secure, ambivalent, avoidant, and disorganized.

Secure attachments are just that—safe. A parent or caregiver who is emotionally available and appropriately responsive to his or her child fosters these loving and secure bonds. People with secure attachments are capable of processing and handling both positive and negative emotions. I did not have a secure attachment with my mother, and a mother is one of the main individuals from which we develop our attachment style.

In my home, my mother provided a toxic kind of love. Her mental health issues contributed to me developing a disorganized attachment style. Disorganized attachment occurs when parents or caregivers mistreat the child, frequently frighten the child, miscommunicate feelings, do not have the capacity to communicate feelings to the child at all, or have highly unrealistic expectations of the child. One main symptom of disorganized attachment is the struggle to receive care. Because my mother didn't care for me, it caused me shame to need care. I harbored humiliation around the fact that I even had needs at all. Today, when someone tries to care for me, it still causes internal panic. Many clinicians and researchers describe people with disorganized attachment as having a "shattered self."

I was faced with the dilemma of both protecting myself from my mother's mental illness (which I didn't yet know about) and trying to create and maintain a relationship with her. Like so many with this type of history, when my initial bond was filled with pain, I believed the pain was the bond. This balancing act was a lot to manage for a child.

In toxic relationships, there is an obsession with trying to change another individual into someone you'd rather they be instead of loving them for who they are. My mother dismissed me because of my appearance. At least that is how I interpreted it as a child. Today, I understand she dismissed me because of her lack of emotional and mental health. But as a little girl, I, like so many other children, was wrapped in shame about how I looked, and truly believed she didn't like me solely based on her opinion of my appearance.

I learned from cues from those around me that since I was female, my job was to be pretty like my mom. I believed I was failing at that job. She dismissed my feelings, never validating me for who I was or what I felt. She didn't love me for me.

When I entered elementary school, my mother starting providing more blatant evidence of her displeasure toward me. In stores or during other outings, strangers would offer compliment after compliment for my handsome brother and elegant mother. No one ever acknowledged me, including my mother. It was as if I wasn't there at all. Actually, it was worse than that because it was my own mother who not only ignored me but also unleashed her own river of criticism for who I was and how I looked.

On one occasion, I was playing with my mother's makeup. As many young girls do, I was trying to look "pretty." But, unlike most girls feel the overwhelming need to do, I was trying desperately to connect with my mother on some level I thought she might understand (perhaps even accept!). I was looking for approval. I was yearning to be able to ask, "Mom, am I pretty?" and for her to say something like, "Of course you're pretty," simply because I was her daughter.

After careful application of the makeup, I excitedly went to find my mother so I could present myself as the masterpiece I was longing to be (and now know I am). Her reaction was not what I had envisioned in my young mind. In fact, she didn't just yell at me, she verbally abused me. I felt so small. Finally I walked away. I hung my head to hide my face, and I went to wash off the makeup, feeling more rejected than ever.

Another day, I was feeling a bit brave, and I asked my mother a question: "What do I have to do to be treated the same as Jimmy and Daddy?"

I was only five years old. In my opinion, it was the last smart question I asked for the next twenty years. I don't remember her response. It doesn't matter. Even as a little girl, I was trying to reconcile the reality that she treated my brother differently than me, and I knew I lived unseen. The fact I had to ask that question speaks volumes about how, at even a young age, I was lost in my own home. I was failing at being a girl. I was not good enough, and no one took the time to change that warped thought-process. I lived lost, and my mother provided no validation that I could ever do anything to be found again.

The lies I believed about what it meant to be female erupted into deep-seeded deceptions with each passing year, especially as I started physically maturing. The researchers and psychologists were correct in their textbook assessments about attachment theory. I was undeniably a "shattered self."

I don't share all this to blame my mother. As a matter of fact, I have my own definition of blame. Blame is one of the main components of emotional paralysis. You cannot blame yourself or someone else and have forward movement. Blame and responsibility are not the same things. I would venture that blame and responsibility have never even met; they don't play on the same playground. Later in my life, God was the One who taught me about responsibility and accountability.

Today, I take responsibility for how my mother's illness affected me, and I give her accountability for being sick. The sickness is hers. Taking responsibility for what I personalized is on me.

While I have been able to repair in this area, I can be easily reminded of toxic love. For example, I was recently standing among a group of friends at church and someone I respected walked up and gave a compliment to everyone but me. That hurt, but I now know I have a voice and can speak up for myself. I've learned it is my responsibility to advocate for the one Jesus saved. But most children, like me, feel they do not have a voice. Imagine that child's own mother being that person in the scenario and that exchange happening every day of her childhood. That was my childhood.

This book was not written as a medium for me to point my finger and have you believe I had no choices when it came to my behavior as I moved into adolescence and beyond. My hope is that you understand the depth of the dysfunctional connection between my mother and me. It was (and is) a defining relationship that deeply affects my life, even as an adult.

CHAPTER 5
CONNECTING WITH ED

Small things start to feel big when, out of shame,
we act like big things are small.

~ KBH

Conversation with My Mother:

Kim: "Mom did you know that red heads always have thick hair?"

Mother: "Your grandmother had thick hair, and she wasn't a red head."

Kim: "Mother, I did not say that all people with thick hair have red hair. I said all redheads have thick hair."

Mother: "Oh well... Do you know how your brother is doing?"

Kim: "He is fine, Mom."

Mother: "Well he came to see his son and didn't come by here on Saturday. I guess he is growing up."

Kim: "He is 44 years old, Mother."

Mother: "I KNOW he is 44! Well, I didn't know his exact age, but I knew he was in his 40's!"

The number of bizarre, thick curls on my head was how many ways I received the message that my mother could not love, accept, or approve of me because I wasn't perceived as pretty. Family members, strangers, children, teachers, and so many others felt the freedom to tell me their opinion regarding my appearance. *Are you a boy or a girl? Either way, you sure are ugly.* Even "compliments" were backhanded insults. *You aren't as ugly as you used to be.*

"What happened to you?" was a common question asked of me when others in the community saw my whole family together. I looked so different from the rest of my family. I kept waiting for my parents to take me into a room, close the door, and tell me that I was adopted. I could have been the poster child for the song on the PBS show *Sesame Street* that goes, "One of these things is not like the other..." I could go on and on, but you get the shame drift.

Even though I grew up in the amazing, gentle, small town of Fort Mill, there were still aggressive bullies. But honestly, I don't know what hurt more—being made fun of by my peers or by my own family members. I think all of us have a bully story, one in which we were bullied, or if we admit it, when we were the bully. Being teased or harassed is a trauma. Since it happens to most of us at some point, it is considered a normalized trauma. Having the word normalized in front of the word trauma is very ironic. I think grammar geeks call that an oxymoron. Now, that is a funny word—

I do know this: People who carelessly attacked my appearance or constantly touched my hair in disbelief took away any sense of normalcy that I had, especially when it was my own family. I was the outlier of the family. I wished I really had been black, or at least "brack." As God's children, we are all born with emotional (relational) needs. They are perfectly normal and necessary. It doesn't mean we are *needy* to yearn for these innate desires; they are by God's design. My need for acceptance went unmet. My need for approval was squashed. And, the emotional security well ran dry very early on in my life.

My mother desperately searched to find someone who could handle genetically mutated hair from Hades. She was embarrassed enough of me (not for me) to want to help. When I was a teenager, she found a woman in Charlotte, North Carolina who said she could tame my mag (hair). I drove excitedly to Charlotte, but I was also full of fear about receiving yet another bad haircut. Even more than that, I was afraid of the scissor sharp comments the hair stylist might make (see what I did there?).

I arrived at the fancy salon and sat quietly in the chair as the stylist examined my bird's nest. Then, she started to laugh.

"What is so funny?" I asked.

"Oh nothing," she quipped. " I am just thanking God for what I have."

To this day, I see a "Hair Therapist." In case you're blessed with the ability to see just any hairdresser, let me explain. My Hair Therapist provides me with not only extra special hair care and taming treatments, but she also understands my deep-rooted (see what I did there again?) hair trauma and steers clear of derogatory comments. My mother knows about my Hair Therapist, and she still dishes out backhanded comments.

In fact just the other day, I mentioned to my mother that I had to find a new Hair Therapist because the one I have been seeing for years was moving out of town. Her oh-so-soothing reply? "Well, your hair did start looking *different* lately."

Recently, I went back and opened my childhood journal. Pain flooded my entire soul as I read, *if only I could do something with my hair, maybe my mom would like me.* I wanted to hug that little girl who was I and tell her that there was a God who adored her.

Even now, there is a small but mighty part of me, deep below the surface, that twists a little (okay, perhaps a lot) when others use gender-specific labels or terms when referring to co-ed audiences. *Man*kind. Hey, *guys*. Fresh*man*. When I hear or read these terms, my inner child comes forth. I have to intentionally fight against the rejection and insignificance that pricks my heart's scars as these feelings bubble toward the surface. A case in point—I threatened my ghostwriter who is typing these very words that if she used any of these terms, I would burn the manuscript and fire her butt.

Feeling so different for the duration of my childhood has given me a mega-sized passion for inclusion. I have a burning desire for our language, laws, and opportunities to avoid excluding people (whether intentional or not) based on their perceived attractiveness, gender, size, race, sexual orientation, and marital status. No one should feel alone.

What happens to you when you are young *does* matter. Appearance is the number one area of shame for women. I was dunked in the cesspool of appearance shame so much that, after awhile, I learned to jump in voluntarily and do the backstroke myself. The roots of shame were growing deeper and stronger.

There are countless stories, but I don't believe there are words adequate enough to describe the environment of my childhood. The difference between something being "traumatic" and a circumstance being a "bad experience" is support. So, what happens to the child who is supposed to receive the most support from the very person who is causing the most harm?

The mounting shame gave birth to a more outward indication of my growing struggles. Not long before Charlie's demise, I had thought I had discovered the single way I might connect with my mother. I learned to find some measure of approval in the area of weight management.

We live in an image-conscious society. Women, especially, are conditioned to believe weight and beauty matter more than God ever intended. My mother took it to the extreme.

My mother had a tendency to disappear at times. It was nothing too drastic like going for a pack of cigarettes and not coming home for a few days. She would just engage in activities such as locking herself in a room for a couple of months to keep from eating. Apparently, I ruined her body while I was growing inside it.

I decided the way to her heart was to lose weight. It didn't matter that I was already at a normal weight for a child my age. I just wanted to be good enough. I didn't have words for my feelings at the time. I wasn't aware of my subconscious and dysfunctional beliefs, nor did I understand from where they stemmed. I only knew that I longed for her to like me, so I did what she did. I chewed gum instead of eating food and exercised as if I was training for the Olympics. If it weren't for school, I would have likely hid in the closet, too.

As a seven-year-old, I was praised for all the exercising, gum chewing, and weight loss. I learned a powerful message about body image. I learned it was important – at least to my family. At one point in my mid-teen years, my mother even bribed me. The deal was that if I lost ten pounds, she would move my curfew an hour later. So of course, I did it. Never mind that it was accomplished by taking illegal drugs!

I learned very quickly that if I stayed skinny, my mother noticed. She finally saw me! That's all it took for me to take the first step up the playground ladder on my way to the top of the slippery slide that I would use to careen down into my first addiction—ED. It's otherwise known as an eating disorder.

People learn to engage in unhealthy behaviors in response to their environment and whether or not their needs are met. In addition, people's thoughts and beliefs directly impact their feelings. This, in turn, determines their behavior. To the extent that someone's thoughts and beliefs are unrealistic or dysfunctional, their behavior will be similarly affected. If your needs are unmet, and particularly if you are shamed for even having emotional needs (the need for attention, the need to be seen), you will go into addictive behavior.

Eating disorders are complex disorders, influenced by a myriad of factors. Though the exact cause of eating disorders is unknown, it is generally believed that a combination of biological, psychological, or environmental "abnormalities" contribute to the development of these illnesses. Well, I would say that as a child, I certainly had a few biological, psychological, and environmental influencers that negatively impacted me. Actor and outspoken recovering alcoholic, Matthew Perry, once said, "The opposite of addiction is connection." I had no connection with my mother and little connection with others.

In elementary school, it was anorexia, perpetuated by my mother's constant dieting. In high school, I started spending food money on liquor, which meant less food. I considered this an added bonus. While ED and I met before I became intimate with Jack Daniels, college was when ED spiraled out of control. In my first year of college, I began purging and my anorexia joined its sibling disease, bulimia, to ensure my food addiction was complete.

In college, a friend and I would drive around town and hit several fast food places, get a hotel room, and then binge-and-purge for hours. One fine example of how my trauma had turned into numbness by this time was when this friend and I jumped out of my car and stood beside each other talking at a gas station on our way to the next destination. I pumped just enough gas to get us where we wanted to go but not enough to "drink" up our beer money. Then, we both heard it. Two guys screamed to get what I thought was *our attention*. I turned around and one of them yelled at me: "Not you! Your friend!" Honestly, this was such a common occurrence that I didn't even feel my soul being pierced. I did what I always did. I drank and purged. I was deep into my recovery many years later before I was able to release this type of pain and shame from my depths.

My disease escalated in my thirties so drastically that I chewed my food to appease those who asked me if I was eating, and then I would spit it in the dog's dish so that I didn't swallow it. When I started my first adult job as a probation officer, I was barely eating at all. As part of my "uniform," I carried a gun. I have no idea who thought that was a wise idea! None-the-less, it was strapped to my scrawny little side. I was so small at the time, people joked that my gun was bigger than me. When I entered the county jails, the inmates would holler, "Hey, skinny b—!" I considered it the greatest compliment they could give me. The attention continued to feed my need to feel seen and be significant.

I had no clue at the time that this behavior was a means of hiding pain. Not so ironically, no one believed I had an eating disorder because it is considered a "pretty woman's disease." I wasn't even good enough to be sick.

I soon realized that this food "issue" complimented my other growing addiction quite well. I learned I could get drunk faster if I was lighter. My pain continued to retreat deep within me with every decision I made to act out through one of my addictions. My self-destructive behavior continued on its seductive march forward. Or, perhaps I should I say down the slippery slope of shame?

CHAPTER 6

HALF SEAS OVER

The most selfish thing you can do is neglect yourself.

~ KBH

t didn't take long for me to ride down the entire slide of self-destruction. My continued pain devastated my life through two symptomatic addictions: eating disorders and alcoholism.

Beginning around age eleven, I became a regular drinker. I say that without much emotion. I know others may stare at me in disbelief when they hear "eleven," but there is no surprise left for me to feel with that statement. Eleven. Most eleven-year-olds are chasing some sport, honing a particular talent, discovering a new skill, or preparing to watch PG13 movies.

It was at my grandmother's house where I had my first taste of alcohol. I was eight years old. At some point, my brother and I were both offered adult beverages each time we visited. He always said no. I always said yes. The amount was controlled and many adults were around us, *supervising*. But something became different for me when I drank.

My response and enthusiasm for alcohol was unparalleled to most others'. At the age of eleven, my parents had a housewarming party just after we moved into our new home in Fort Mill. At this party, I discovered that adults did bizarre things like set their drinks down and turn away from them. I would "taste test" their beverages while they were otherwise engaged. Okay, I flat out stole sips (gulps) of liquor from unsuspecting adults that evening. This consumption was in addition to the small amounts I was being afforded anyway.

Not surprisingly, since I was a mere child, I became highly intoxicated. Throughout the evening, I would "come to" and find myself speaking to my uncle or my brother and not know how I got to that particular room or managed to engage them in the conversations we were having!

In the blink of an eye, it was morning and not only was there an impressive trail of vomit from my bed to my bathroom, there was also the mystery of how I ended up in my bathtub. What was not mysterious to me was that my mother was looming over my hungover body and screaming at me. She had a right to be indignant. Her young daughter was intoxicated to the level of vomiting and waking up from her first blackout—at age eleven. But she always screamed at me; hence, there was no mystery.

Her level of outrage matched my level of relief. As I stared at her, I realized I had found what I had been looking for my whole short life. I had stumbled across (literally) the remedy that propelled me from "never good enough" to believing I was, in fact, good enough. I was unaware that I had not actually shed my shame. I had simply placed a thin veil over it. I had no idea I would continue to abuse myself worse than my mother ever had in the years to come. All I knew in that moment in the bathtub was that the condescending voices in my head singing "you're not good enough" were quiet. My mother's screams ricocheted in my ears and did nothing to hurt me. I had no feelings about them at all. That was what I had been seeking for quite some time—a reprieve from all those negative thoughts and emotions.

For the next 4,383 days, I continued to drink.

In the midst of that long season, I believed the most ridiculous of lies. I thought that I wouldn't have any friends—particularly no dates or boyfriends—if I didn't drink. I assumed that, somehow, the alcohol hid my unattractiveness. The irony of that statement is almost too much to bear now.

In junior high (or middle school, depending on where and when you grew up), I learned a great deal about marijuana and added that to my menu of pain-hiding recipes. After that, I tried cocaine. I was a daily drinker or partaker in any number of controlled substances by eighth grade. I was sent to my first outpatient facility in eighth grade after getting caught with the drug called speed. It didn't work. By ninth grade, I was doing whatever I could to avoid feeling anything.

I was an average or above average student for the most part, securing a majority of A's and B's from elementary school through high school. I was tremendously disciplined. I credit my father for giving me his intellectual genes and my mother for making sure most of our toys were educational ones. I did fairly well academically, even when alcohol was all that mattered to me. However, after being released from my first in-patient treatment center during my junior year of high school, I realized I needed to get my priorities straight. So I went to the library and then I went to the bar. Makes perfect sense, doesn't it?

One day, I sat my daddy down to tell him I was dropping out of school so I could party. As a wise attorney's daughter, I tempered my plea with the argument that I was not going to go to college anyway. Well. Let's just say I received such a strong verbal lashing from my daddy that day that I knew I was going to college no matter what.

On the first day of high school, I woke up overwhelmed with anxiety. At school, an older student asked me if I ever got high. "Of course I do," I retorted, and before I knew it, I was in my new "friend's" car, and we were on our way to the local bootleggers' house.

Let me tell you about the bootleggers. They were a geriatric couple that lived in a small house. Of course, when you're fourteen, geriatric can mean thirty years old, but I really think they were in their seventies. What I do know is they had a plethora of pints of liquor, and I had a healthy liver to destroy. They were a sweet, gentle people who would, without hesitation, sell me a pint of Lord Calvert for $6.00! At times, my friends and I would leave school during lunch to get a pint, and at other times, I would stock up so I could drink before and after school.

On one particular Friday in high school, something new happened in the little town of Fort Mill. It started as a normal school day, which means either before school or during lunch, I visited the bootleggers. Either way, I had enough alcohol coursing through my body to be able to talk to anyone without a care in the world. On this day, a new boy had shown up in our Physical Education (P.E.) class. His name was Brian. All my classmates and I were huddled on the butt-numbing bleachers surrounding this poor new kid. We were curious. We had a lot of questions. He informed the mob gathered around him that he was from Soddy Daisy, Tennessee. I really don't think the Fort Mill school district taught geography. Tennessee seemed as foreign and distant to us as Africa.

At any rate, Brian then let us in on a little secret. He said he was the "son of Satan." My classmates became like cockroaches and scattered faster than you can say "Soddy Daisy." Not me. I stayed, because I was intrigued.

When I arrived home from school that day, I walked in the door and my mom cussed me out as usual. I don't remember what I had done wrong. I just knew this time, I had a new friend to contact. I called up Brian, and he told me his little brother was still in Tennessee. We conjured up a plan to go see him. I stole some money from my parents, picked up Brian in my 1981 Honda Prelude, and I ran away for the first time in my life. I was fifteen.

When we arrived in Tennessee the next morning, I called home—collect, of course. My mother answered the phone. The only thing I said was, "I'm not dead." She wasn't amused.

"Who gave you permission to run away?"

She had not come looking for me. We were a family of independent and autonomous individuals. We did not eat dinner together or anything like that. Eventually, late the previous night, they had all realized I was gone. When I called my mother, my daddy had been on the streets of Fort Mill looking for me for hours. She had stayed home.

"Why are you doing this?" my mother asked after I informed her I wasn't dead. I didn't tell her where I was, and I didn't voluntarily return. My parents traced the collect call, and I was forced to return home. So, Brian and I drove back to North Carolina. We were home before school started on Monday. The response I received from each member of my family was no surprise to me. My brother, Golden Boy, was frustrated because I had taken all of Dad's money, and he had wanted some of it to go out with his girlfriend. (It would be years before I realized that I had also hurt my brother with my choices.) My dad cried. My mother was emotionally detached and seemingly unaffected. Her lack of love or concern for her runaway daughter was one more line item on the long list of rejections.

Conversation with My Mother:

Kim: "Hey, Mom."

Mother: "Kim, I have a question for you."

Kim: "Okay, go for it."

Mother: "Did I verbally abuse you when you were growing up?"

Kim: "What do you think, Mother?"

Mother: "Yes. Yes, I think I did."

Kim: "Well, I agree. I don't remember a whole lot, but I remember you hiding from us when we were very little."

Mother: "Well, it was a small house. You could have found me if you had tried."

My relationship with the bootleggers ended about a year after it started. One day, I went to see them. I sat at the gentleman's card table (I mean, dining room table), and he told me it was going to be the last time he would sell to me.

"Wait, what? Why?"

"Now, Kim, there are some people who can drink and there are some who can't."

"Yeah, okay. That's cool, but what does that have to do with me?"

"Some people can't control their liquor. You are one of those people. We don't want to sell to you anymore.

The only way I can describe the look on my face while I sat at that table is if you have ever watched the television show, *The Office*, you've seen the look Jim always gives Michael Scott. My focus quickly turned to how I could find my next supplier. I didn't feel the need to understand the reason he wouldn't sell to me.

Or, maybe I just wasn't ready to comprehend.

CHAPTER 7

THE FALL

It is not the event that tethers you to pain.
It is the false belief that comes from the painful event.

~ KBH

Soon after the bootleggers cut me off, I finished ninth grade. My math grade was so fabulous that I was invited to take Algebra in summer school. (I hope you are reading the term *fabulous* with as much sarcasm as I intended.) After all, who can do math when they're constantly drunk or high? I was still fifteen years old. The math I was passionate about learning included dime bags of marijuana and eight balls of cocaine. I knew how to count enough diet pills to make the number on the scale reflect the person my mother wanted me to be. Actual math, well—seemed blah.

The summer class was more advanced than the one I failed, but the concepts seemed to come more naturally to me. I was even asked to tutor the other kids in the class! Unfortunately I couldn't translate all that wonderful information in my head onto a test very well. Can anyone say, ADHD (Attention Deficit Hyperactive Disorder)? Anyway, as a reward for doing well (aside from that final test), my dad gave me permission to go to Myrtle Beach, South Carolina with a friend. Myrtle Beach is a touristy ocean-side town where the kids from Fort Mill used to go at the conclusion of each school year and where many college kids go for Spring Break. Families go, too, thinking it's a nice vacation locale.

I was there for about four hours before *it* happened. I remember only the first two hours of this short-lived vacation. My friend and I found other teens from the Fort Mill area to hang out with as soon as we arrived. We were invited to a hotel room party. Of course we said yes, and after greeting some friends, I started drinking and sniffing rush (a drug of choice at the time).

I do not remember my hand wrapped around the wine cooler as I hoisted myself onto the railing of the hotel's balcony. Apparently, my aim was not as accurate as one might hope when jumping onto such a narrow rail, and I spiraled right off the balcony. Witnesses watched me land head first on the cement two stories below. The wine cooler shattered next to me on the pavement.

Two other friends from Fort Mill who just happened to be walking by came upon my motionless body. As I later learned, they tried their best to comfort me until an ambulance arrived. I have no recollection of these moments. For that, I am grateful.

As a side note that details this experience, after many years had passed, one of the people who found me on the pavement sent me a message on Facebook (and some people think Facebook is bad!). He shared with me how traumatic it was to see someone he had known since before Kindergarten so badly incapacitated. There were many kids (and parents) who were aware of my drinking, so for him to see my body with a bottle smashed beside it was overwhelming for him.

Sadly, it was going to be years before I would be able to comprehend how any of my actions impacted others. It wouldn't be until sobriety when I would finally realize my self-neglect actually made things more about me and less about others. Not the real me, mind you. Destruction distracted me from my pain but also from whom I really was; it had me believing I was as good as my last drunk. It was never my intention, but it was a by-product of my addiction. I hated myself and assumed everyone else did as well, so

I did not understand how my actions could possibly affect others. My foundational thought was *my own mother doesn't love me, so why would anyone else be impacted by my life and choices?*

Back to the fall...I regained consciousness and immediately knew I was not able to move my head. I slowly moved my eyes to the left. My father stood there beside a hospital bed. I gradually realized it was *my* hospital bed. A priest and two nuns were on the right side of my bed. I appreciate this may be starting to sound like a bad joke, perhaps one that should be told at a bar as people sit shoulder to shoulder while slamming tequila shots, but this really did happen. I had been rushed to Grand Strand Hospital and admitted into the intensive care unit.

When I awoke and saw my dad, the priest, and the two nuns, I was confused and had no idea how much time had elapsed. I did know the look on my father's face was not one I had seen often. I turned to look at the priest and nuns, trying desperately to absorb the significance of their presence and comprehend the priest's words. I darted my eyes back at my father and asked, "What are they doing?"

"They are reading you your last rites," my father replied, his eyes sad. Still hazy and confused, I failed to understand that my dad had received the phone call that every parent hopes to never get. I didn't know that he and my Uncle Joe had raced from Fort Mill to Myrtle Beach, South Carolina at lightning speed, not knowing if they would find me alive or not. I was unaware that the doctors told my exhausted and worried father upon his arrival that his little girl had a fifty percent chance of living, and that if I did survive, I would likely have partial paralysis in my face. (How ironic would that have been?) I had no knowledge that my skull was fractured or that I had a blood clot near my brain. I was too sedated to feel the staples holding my flesh in place. All I knew was that, while not suicidal, I didn't really want to live. Without any understanding of the power of my words in God's grand plan, I looked at my daddy, and I responded, "Tell them to stop."

On the seventh day of my hospital stay, my mother came to visit me. My father had been there within hours of the accident, but my mother had remained at home for a week. She visited with me for thirty minutes after her three-hour car ride and then simply stood up and claimed she had to go. Her excuse was that an elderly woman had traveled with her, and she couldn't just leave her in the car. After all, that would be rude. The feeling of rejection flooded me. (Another side note: To this day, no one, including my mother, knows who this woman in the car was. If she comes forward, I will give her a million dollars. Though, don't hold me to that number.)

My father was there in the hospital. My Uncle Joe had come with him. A team of medical professionals was caring for me. A priest and two nuns were by my side. The woman whom I had known the longest and who carried me until I entered this world would not stay with me. There are few words adequate enough to express the hurt that enveloped me in that hospital bed, and I'm not referring to the physical pain. The rejection was an extra bed sheet, tucked under every inch of my broken body, not for comfort or warmth, but rather holding me down. In fact, that sheet had been holding me down for so long that I barely acknowledged it.

I now know the Good News of those moments. The God I didn't even know yet (but who knew me since before conception) was there. The One who knit me together in my mother's womb was beside me. I didn't embrace the irony and beauty of this fact for many years. If I use my heart's eye to look back, I can find Him on the cement pavement. I can see Him in the hospital room. I can sense His constant and loving grace. I have a Heavenly Father whose love and presence completely fill and sustain me. Today, as I reflect on the enormous sense of aloneness and abandonment I felt during that time, knowing He was there with me through the physical and the emotional hurts, comforts me.

However, it would be a long time before I would be able to understand all this. In that hospital room, I abandoned myself. I hurt myself. In my mind, I recreated what she did to me in a way that helped me think I was in charge of it all. I needed to feel powerful, because I was in my greatest moment of vulnerability with no one to make me feel safe. I abused myself to avoid feeling the pain of the one who abused me first.

CHAPTER 8

THE DRY CAMPUS

Blame is what happens when I place more fault on myself or
on God than the situation warrants.

~ KBH

After surviving the fall that should have terminated my existence, I returned home. I wish the close call had been my wake-up call. It wasn't.

Less than two years later, at the age of seventeen, my dad gave me a new car. She was black with T-tops, and I loved her. I do have an affinity for cars, which I must have acquired from Golden Boy. Soon after I received my amazing hot rod, I agreed to go into a treatment center to address my excessive drinking. I was a junior in high school. My grades were adequate, and I was involved in many (legal) extracurricular activities, one of which was the track team. Yet, everything was put on hold, and I was placed in an adult inpatient center called Charlotte Treatment Center (CTC).

My stay at CTC was not successful. The treatment team called in an outside psychiatrist to administer additional psychological testing. I must not have done well. Soon after, I was pulled into a room with the intimidating treatment team. It was an intervention meeting. It was here that I was told I was too emotionally unstable to remain at CTC. I thought, *No crap! Have you met my mother?* Picture "Jim" from the television show *The Office* and the way he looks away when Michael Scott says something ridiculous. That was my countenance at the intervention meeting. Every patient seemed emotionally immature. That is part of the disease of alcoholism. Apparently though, I was the worst, so I was asked to leave. You can guess who came to my rescue. Yep, my sweet daddy! He picked me up and whisked me home.

There was one outrageous outcome from my stay at CTC. While I was a patient, it was time for me to complete the SAT application. I was experiencing physical withdrawal from alcohol, but I believe what happened next was not my mistake but rather my Heavenly Father's intervention (see what I did there?). Again, the One Whom I knew nothing about was once again extending His grace to me.

Let me start with a cold, hard fact. Everyone in my family attended the University of South Carolina. My dad completed his undergraduate work at this fine institution of higher learning and received his Juris Doctorate from USC as well. I was fixated on following in his and my brother's footsteps. When the SAT application asked me to choose where I wanted my scores sent, I mistook Columbia College (CC) for USC. I saw Columbia College but thought it was USC. Yeah, yeah I know; I already told you I wasn't in the best frame of mind. Anyway, as it turned out, Columbia College is an all women's college that just happens to be a Christian school. God was setting up a divine introduction between He and I.

Not long after that, Columbia College started sending me information. Quite honestly, I didn't have a lot of higher education options. Most schools wouldn't take a risk with me. Part of the reason is a bit embarrassing. Since that hasn't stopped me from sharing in the past, I won't start now. If you're older than three or four decades, you may remember the magic score for the SAT college entrance exam was 1600. Well, my score was...*Okay, spit it out, Kim.* Pep talks are awesome, people! Okay. Let's put it this way: My credit score today is much higher than my SAT score back in the day. It was a score that you would not want to write home about. Certainly not if you were addressing that letter to my mother!

My dad and I planned a visit to Columbia College (CC). The mascot for CC is the Fighting Koala. If you're looking for a sarcastic remark here, there is none to make. The name speaks for itself.

Once on campus, we met the President of the College, Peter Mitchell. He asked me about which major I was interested in pursuing. I said with confidence that it would be Special Education. He replied that my selection was a fine choice and that Columbia College could truly help me prepare for a successful future. Neither Mr. Mitchell nor I had any idea of how prophetic his words would prove to be.

I had two gifts now—the return gift of my alcohol-induced numbness and a new gift I found on the campus of this small Christian college in South Carolina: acceptance. The rejection I experienced from CTC gave me permission to keep drinking. Despite the numbness that my return to the daily intake of alcohol gave me, I felt something new, unusual, and quite special as I toured the campus of CC. I experienced a significant measure of acceptance from a group of people I did not even know. It was a novel feeling. Something was different there. The best analogy I could make at the time was chugging a beer through a funnel at a party and everyone cheering for me. For a moment, I felt like I mattered. Here was a campus full of people, and no one knew my jaded past. Everyone I met provided an encouraging remark, a smile, and a tablespoon full of authentic community. I realized they cheered for everyone, no matter who they were or what they had done. I probably would have been more comfortable if they had truly been fighting koalas but instead they were loving ones, and I had a taste of something distinctive and warm ... something different than the warmth of a smooth whiskey.

Soon after the visit to CC (not USC), I entered my senior year in high school in August. A few months later, on Christmas Eve morning, I totaled my sleek black T-top car on the way home from a motel.

Much like my topple off the railing at the beach, I do not remember the accident at all. What I do recall is regaining consciousness in a hospital and once again seeing my dad standing beside the hospital bed. However, there was one substantial difference. There were no nuns or priests on the other side of my bed. This time, it was a police officer. He was not reading me my last rites; he was reading me my Miranda rights.

I was seventeen years old. I was still a daddy's girl. Here, in front of my father in a hospital room, I was arrested for driving under the influence of alcohol and for refusing to take a Breathalyzer test. My father, who was (and is) known in our small town as "Gentle Jim," had to watch helplessly as a Highway Patrol Trooper arrested his little girl.

My daddy didn't love me any differently after that, but my love for myself dwindled to almost nothing the longer and deeper my alcoholism progressed. My car was totaled. I had embarrassed and hurt the most important person in my life, and all I knew to do was drink. Even when there were strikingly significant consequences for my addiction, I couldn't stop drinking. I had secretly contacted several support groups, but I never followed through with them. The pain of the consequences from my alcoholism was so strong for me that all I knew to do was to participate in the behavior that caused the pain in the first place. So, I drank. And then I drank some more.

Several months later, on my 18th birthday (March 12—mark your calendars now), I came home to find a new beautiful, silky, black car. There was a Nissan 240sx parked in front of the house. I knew it was for me, and I knew it was from my dad. As if that wasn't special enough, there was a letter from Columbia College taped to the steering wheel. I was hesitant to open the letter. I knew I wouldn't be able to handle a rejection. The look of confidence in my father's eyes encouraged me.

"Open it," he whispered. "It's okay."

So I did. It was an acceptance letter. In that moment, I recognized how appropriately named an "acceptance" letter is for so many people. I felt chosen. I did not realize how much more poignant that feeling of acceptance would become once I arrived at CC. I was on the verge of starting college—a new phase of my life—at a school that would accept me exactly as I was but also encourage me to be even more.

I didn't get to drive my brand new vehicle for long. While I was grateful for the acceptance letter from Columbia College, I also received a letter from the South Carolina Department of Motor Vehicles. They wanted me to know my license had been revoked for ninety days for refusing to submit to the Breathalyzer test on Christmas Eve morning.

The calendar flipped to June. With my revoked license, I couldn't drive to my high school graduation. Instead, I showed up thirty minutes late, drunk, and sat in the stands to watch my friends (whom I'd known since pre-school) walk across the field and receive their diplomas. I observed, motionless and paralyzed by sadness and the numbing effects of intoxication. I sat there too inebriated to know the significance of how I had just rejected myself in the very way others had been rejecting me my whole life. Interesting enough, this is one of the bigger moments I regret in life. Sadly, I cannot undo or redo that special day.

Conversation with My Mother:

Mother: "Something terrible happened yesterday."

Kim: "What happened?"

Mother: "The interior designer was 35, maybe 40 minutes late yesterday."

Kim: "So what terrible thing happened yesterday? (I really thought I missed something.)

Mother: "The designer was late, and I couldn't hold back my anger."

Kim: "Well being late is disrespectful but no one died, there was no injury, no assault; but, I understand she wasted your time."

Mother: "Well that is one way to look at it. I can't decide exactly what to get Regan for her birthday. (Regan is my niece.) So I told your dad to Google what 14-year-old girls like."

Kim: "Yeah, Mom, that's really not a good idea to have that on dad's work computer. Really, really might want to reword that."

My first day at Columbia College was the day my driver's license was reinstated. After my suspension, there I sat in the driver's seat of my black Nissan 240sx heading off to college while my parents followed me. I was eighteen and had been a daily drinker for about seven years now. I showed up on campus with quite a history. I had been in treatment for alcoholism, been arrested, run away from home, and endured a fall that had left me with a fifty percent chance of survival. In addition to all of that, I showed up at Columbia College to move in as a first year student donning a lovely cast because I had put my fist through a window while drunk. The doctors couldn't tell me if I would ever regain full use of my hand.

I was the antithesis of those around me. The young women I saw on the campus of Columbia College looked perfect. They all seemed to have impeccable hair (you can now appreciate why I noticed that first), flawless makeup, and adorable outfits. They had names like Happy, Kappy, and Muffin. I saw them lugging suitcase after suitcase into their dorm rooms, and every young lady seemed to be hemorrhaging shoes. I had one pair. They were on my feet.

If I had not been numb with alcohol, I likely would have left. Strangely, there was also a deep-down portion of me that felt a sense of belonging at Columbia College, despite the fact that I was obviously different than most of my peers. Looking back, I can say without hesitation that I had no inkling on that first day how crucial this institution was about to be in my life. I just knew I was already starting to feel different.

The school had not been my first choice. However, it was His choice for me. Perhaps that was why I felt it might work out; God's hands were directing my path. The fact that I didn't know Him or serve Him never swayed Him from loving me. Imagine that!

I watched while parents held onto their daughters after helping them move in before heading back home. They were all crying. I watched them with the same bewildered expression I would have had if I had watched a movie in Japanese. They were not speaking any language I knew or really cared to know. This clingy, pitiful display of love was not the scene that played out with my parents and me. There were no tearful goodbyes; my father slipped me some money, and then my parents and brother (yes, he came too) left. It was swift and simple, and I am sure I was as relieved as they were in the knowledge we would never again see each other daily.

While all the preppy girls were introducing themselves and unpacking, I headed out to get a 12-pack. I wasn't upset or bothered in the least to be on my own. I was grateful. My family had dropped me off at an expensive school, and I was free from my mother's disapproving rants. All I knew (and needed to know) on that first day was that I could drink. That's what people do in college—they drink, right? I figured I would look normal and fit in for perhaps the first time in my life.

A month into the first semester, I finally called home. Yes, I was the one who took the initiative. It was time; I missed my dad. My mother answered the phone and straightforwardly informed me, "You don't need to call here. No one here wants to talk to you."

The relational separation between us quickly ripped through the phone and sliced my heart but then just as quickly left again. Alcohol was always good for silencing the pain and hurtful voices. It would numb this moment, too.

One day, I perused the student directory and found myself in the listings of first year students. Well, my name was there. Since I was too insecure to get in front of a camera, I had never submitted a photo. In its place was the image of our mascot, the Fighting Koala. It was staring at me. What was really freaky, though, was that underneath my name, my major was listed. *Psychology*. I was so shocked that I exclaimed aloud, "Huh? I didn't know that!"

I went with it. I attended the classes that would satisfy that degree rather than the Special Education degree. Today, I know it was my God who had decided I needed to attend Columbia College and major in psychology. Back then, the only time I would say His name was in vain, like when I saw flashing blue lights behind me. All I knew was self-hatred and alcoholism. He loved me anyway. He pursued me anyway. He was directing my path when I couldn't do it myself. I made it official and declared my major, went to my classes, and of course, I drank. Everything was as normal as I could be and feel—

—until I got caught. Columbia College is a dry campus, and there was a student-run Judicial Council in place to enforce the rules.

I had met some really amazing and adventure-loving friends, and we were sitting around in my room with a case of beer and twelve bottles of liquor.

Knock! Knock! Knock! One of my friends opened the door to find the chairperson of the Judicial Council and her entourage ready to storm the room. We were definitely in trouble.

Within a couple weeks, my friends and I were forced to appear in front of the council to explain our actions. I don't remember what I said in my defense. It probably didn't matter.

There was a long delay for the verdict to be rendered. We found out later that I was, in fact, the reason for the hold up. The students who had been elected to the council were ready to deliver our consequences, but one student had reservations and confided in the council that she thought I had a serious problem. Apparently, word had spread about my "love" for alcohol, and some of my not-so-stellar history from high school was shared. It didn't help that my nickname around campus was "Lush."

The members of the Judicial Council didn't want to just discipline me; they wanted to help me. They showed me mercy and grace when I certainly didn't deserve it. In their final ruling, I was restricted to campus for three weeks and sent to see the school counselor. Her name was Mitzi Winesett, and she turned out to be yet another divine gift. She was not only the college counselor but also a woman who lived with passion and loved with compassion every day and for everyone—including me.

Of course, I didn't realize that right away. I was frustrated that I was being forced to talk to her. Our meetings began soon after my "indictment," and the irony of having to learn how to live without alcohol from a woman whose last name started with "wine" was not lost on me. Maybe that slice of humor prompted me to soften my disdain around her, or maybe it was her ability to listen to my story without emitting one ounce of judgment. Whatever it was that allowed me to share portions of my past with her, I am forever grateful. For it was her love and compassion that began to chip away at the many layers of hatred in which I had encased myself to protect my own hardened heart and yellowing liver.

CHAPTER 9
THE GRADUATE

When God owns you, your circumstances don't.

~ KBH

Mitzi Winesett and I continued to meet regularly for months. In fact, she gave me what turned out to be a prophetic nickname—"Wounded Healer." Because of the rapport we had developed with each other, I agreed to attend Narcotics Anonymous (NA) meetings when she suggested it.

She gave me an NA meeting schedule and promptly acquired the necessary permission from the powers-that-be for me to leave campus. There was a stipulation; Another student, clean and in recovery, had to accompany me.

Mitzi believed that since I was still relatively young, I would relate more with the people in NA rather than those in AA (Alcoholics Anonymous). At the time, it was generally believed that certain drugs—like cocaine—affected the same negative impact in six months what it might take alcohol ten years to do. Since I had been struggling in my addiction for many years, NA seemed to be the better choice.

Mitzi, unlike so many others up to this point, believed in me and hoped I would connect with the people in NA. She wanted me to focus on the similarities we shared, rather than the differences I always seemed to uncover in all my relationships. I now believe that was one of the reasons I had failed to stop drinking so many times before. I had become conditioned to see all the disparities around me—the ways I didn't fit in. It was time to start building connections. I faithfully attended the meetings and, at some point, began to maintain a few periods of sobriety.

As I navigated my first three years at college, I grew in experience and knowledge but, unfortunately, not continued sobriety. There was the instance when I showed up to class only to be directed back home to my dorm room by the professor who didn't want to teach someone who was obviously drunk. There was the other time when I returned to campus completely inebriated after an entire night out and realized I was walking right past my co-eds who were responsibly heading to their morning classes.

Those are minor bad moments. There were much worse experiences, too. There was the day I remember being on campus, but then my next coherent recollection was waking up in Myrtle Beach, naked, in a trailer, and on a man's lap. I figured there was no need to introduce myself. I also recall agreeing to go with a friend to her first Al-Anon meeting. Al-Anon is a support group for people worried about others with a drinking problem. I told her to meet me in the cafeteria, and we'd go together. I showed up drunk.

I was a mess. Yet, I was somehow able to connect with people and present myself as someone who was capable of more than met the eye. During my eventful journey through my years at Columbia College, I advanced from appearing in front of the Judicial Council as a first year student to being voted the chairperson of the Judicial Council in my senior year. It must have been my charming personality. After all, I was still drinking!

On May 8, 1993, I made the mistake of graduating from Columbia College. Despite the connections I had made in NA, my forays into sobriety, and my new status as a graduate of an educational institution I had grown to love and respect, I was still a daily drinker. There was really good news, though. I had shown up that first day of college feeling defeated; I didn't leave that way. I had found some measure of hope. Still only 22 years old, I was departing the only place where I had ever found acceptance. There was a handful of people who believed in me. But I still didn't know how to not drink.

Conversation with My Mother:

Mother: "Hello!"

Kim: "Hey, Mom."

Mother: "Why are you calling me?"

Kim: "Well, I just had a funny feeling and wanted to make sure all is well in the big town of Fort Mill."

Mother: "It is fine, but I have been thinking about you all day."

Kim: (with great excitement) "REALLY, MOM? That is wonderful news. And, guess what? I have been thinking about you all day as well. That means we finally have something in common?"

Mother: "Well, now you made me angry. I have been thinking about you because I want you to look up a certain college address and send it to me."

And mother-daughter moment is over. She wants information that is completely related to and all about her

other child. You know about whom I'm talking—my awesome
big brother. Jimmy Jimmy Jimmy.

As a little girl I would get the court manuscripts from my father and read them with the same fervor that I would later use toward my drinking. I had wanted to be an attorney. I loved the law and my father.

However, I did not go directly to law school upon my graduation. Instead, I was hired as a probation and parole agent in South Carolina. Yes, more irony. My consumption of alcohol didn't decrease even though the magnitude of my responsibilities did. During my stint as a probation and parole agent, I hit one of many lowest of all the low points.

When you are such an agent, you must know where your gun is at all times. I left the office one Friday afternoon with the knowledge that my gun was safely tucked into my vehicle's glove compartment.

I had maintained contact with many college friends. One of my closest friends, Jennie[1] had secured her first teaching job and like an adult, purchased a house in Columbia, South Carolina not far from the campus where we had spent the last four years.

My college roommate, Christy, and I decided to visit Jennie that Friday afternoon to admire her new home. We were excited to see each other and share about our new jobs and lives post college. Of course, we did what college alumnae do when they visit with each other—we went bar hopping. I did what alcoholics do and became extremely intoxicated. This time, it was beyond bad. In one drunken stupor, I became everything I had ever hated.

I left the bar to go find people who were homeless because in my intoxication, I thought they would accept me just as I was. Jennie

---

1   All friends' names changed

and Christy drove around Columbia until they found me staggering down one of the streets. After much coaxing on their parts, I slid into the backseat of my own car. Christy drove and Jennie told her how to get to her house. In my alcohol-induced paranoia, I mistakenly thought they were plotting to kill me. In the backseat, I planned my defense and decided offense was the best tactic. I thought, *I don't want to live but I am not giving them the satisfaction of killing me.* As Christy pulled in front of Jennie's house, I lunged into the front seat and opened the glove compartment. I was determined to use my gun to defend myself from their "murderous plot."

I fumbled around in the glove box and found nothing. For the first and only time, I had left my gun at the office. *An officer always knows where her gun is.* The God I didn't know yet had again reached down from Heaven that day to intervene. Christy and Jennie were frightened by my attempt to find my revolver and even more unnerved when I entered Jennie's house and opened a fresh Budweiser. Jennie knocked the beer out of my hand. She was disgusted that one minute I was ready to aim a gun at her and in the next, I was aiming to ingest more alcohol. In response, I violently turned on her. I only remember pieces of my insanity but I remember enough to know I became a monster.

We struggled, moving from the kitchen to the front door. I pinned her to the ground and repeatedly punched her. Not quite satisfied, I stood up, turned, and began destroying parts of her home. I knocked her CD collection (which had been meticulously alphabetized) to the floor and ripped her personal treasures off tables and shelves. Christy entered the room after ending a phone call in another part of the house and forced me into my car. She quickly drove me home.

I woke up the next day, not recalling exactly what I had done or said to my friends. Though, I remembered enough of the night to wish I had not awakened at all. I spoke with Christy who had called to check on me. Christy divulged to me that I had attempted to find my gun in the glove compartment. I was horrified. I made a promise to myself that morning that I would never drink again. And this time, I meant it.

I was devastated to learn of my actions. Yet again, I had hurt people close to me; hurt those to whom I had promised months earlier that I would stop drinking so much. Still, I had initiated a physical altercation with one good friend and terrified the other. I kept mumbling to myself throughout the day, "Never again. Never again."

By the end of the day, I had a drink in my hand.

CHAPTER 10

THE BOTTOM (STOP IT)

Then one day I decided to stop fighting against myself;
instead, I surrendered to the One who had already won the
war for me, and my life slowly started to change.

~ KBH

Conversation with My Mother:
Well after a sabbatical, Mother called this morning to say:
Mother: "You asked me to think about if I'm mean to you,
and I thought about it. I'm not mean. I'm your mother, not your
friend."
There you have it, folks. That is about as warm as it gets for us.

Needless to say, my life continued to spiral further out of control
and with it went any last feelings of self-worth and hope. On April 1,
1995, not quite two years after I harmed my friend, Jennie, I awoke
again in a place different from where my last memory had placed me.

This time, it was at Mercy Horizons Detox Center in Charlotte, North Carolina. It turned out that on the previous evening, I had become heavily intoxicated and reached out to a few people in an AA group I had known. They cared enough to take me straight to a medical detox facility.

I knew I would not be able to drink there, so I made the impulsive and naïve decision to leave. I walked myself out the door, but it would not be for long. After appraising my life over the previous years, I was nearly ready to admit that I was not a controlled drinker. I was inches away from the proverbial first step towards healing—admitting I had a problem.

Waking up at Mercy Horizons on April Fools' Day was certainly not the first time I had landed in the swampland of shame, remorse, and extreme consequences. But, this time I asked the God I didn't even know (but hoped was there) to remove me from the marshy pit. I knew my own resources and thinking had been unsuccessful. I had always believed in God, and I began praying He would help me. I prayed, even though I did not feel worthy of His help or His love.

I was in incredible emotional pain. God had been patient with me, and over the years He had been planting seeds of wisdom that would grow and help me realize that alcohol could no longer be a solution to my pain. I was slowly realizing my "best friend" was now my abuser, and for the same reason victims of abuse struggle to leave their abusive relationships, I could not imagine life without alcohol. I was becoming increasingly overwhelmed and confused, so I decided to talk to the most influential and intelligent man in my life—my dad.

My father is a self-made man. He is the oldest of seven boys and local folklore says he hitchhiked to college. He still enjoys sharing many stories that seem to involve snow, hills, and mounds of resiliency. However, he does not share any authentic story with me that truly holds pain for him. His facial expressions and the tone of his voice almost always convey calmness and faith. There are people like me who scream about our faith—holy megaphones, if you will—and there are those who walk quietly and simply display faith in motion. My father is a man of movement, and ironically for a lawyer, he is not one of many words.

I went over to my parents' house, and as we usually did, Daddy and I sat outside on the steps. It was our *place*. As I poured out my 24-year-old heart to him, it was obvious that the idea of his little girl needing to depend on someone else to stop drinking was illogical to him. He didn't know the whole story. I was too ashamed to tell him all that I had been through or how many times I had attempted to abstain from alcohol to only feel more disabled. My dad tried to encourage me, reminding me that he raised me to be independent and that I could do this without involving others. I knew deep within me this was the one time my father was wrong; I needed help. He couldn't see the whole picture. I knew his way wouldn't work this time. I had no way of knowing that surrender always involved His (capital "H") way; not the ways of people, no matter how much they loved me. I told my dad I needed medical assistance. Period.

We decided not to involve my mother. Telling her would be like telling Helen Keller you moved the furniture around. It's important for her to know, but you also know the change would cause her to stumble. It would be almost two decades before my mother and I discussed my hospitalization and rehabilitation.

Conversation with My Mother:
Kim: "Mother, my birthday is this month! It's March 1st! Twelve more days!"

Mother: "Uh huh. What do you want for your birthday?"

> Kim: "I want cash."
> Mother: "That works. I don't like shopping in the month of March."

A few weeks later, I approached my supervising agent at work. I explained I needed time off to get help for my drinking. He and I decided that when I left, he'd tell everyone I had pneumonia. We knew people would believe that justification since I looked so sickly. I was still struggling with food-related addictions, and my weight was well below normal (and I wish it still was). Finally, I knew the *how*. I just had to decide the *when*.

April 7, 1995 would be my last "hoorah" party. I was finally ready. I had stood up to my father, told my boss I would be gone for awhile, and announced to friends that I was in agreement with them that I was truly sick and in need of help.

One of my friends took me to the ABC store to let me purchase as much liquor as I wanted for my last drinking party. Of course I had been drinking since I woke up that morning, so by mid-afternoon, I was already a little "toasty." I whispered to my friend as we climbed back into her car with my new stash in the trunk and a Rolling Rock beer in my hand, "If only I could stay right here at this buzz level. If only I could stay right here." I murmured this even as I took another gulp of my beer.

I had agreed with my long-time and super patient friend, Christy, a couple days before this big party that I would go back to the hospital to detox. But, Alcohol didn't want me to. He breathed into my ear, "No one is expecting you at work for a week. You have some cash. Your drinking isn't all that bad. Keep going."

You shouldn't be surprised as I tell you now that I listened to the voice of my alcoholism. It didn't even have to speak loudly. It was so close to me that a whisper was all it took. I was ensnared yet again.

At the party, I tested my new idea about simply taking some time away rather than getting the help I desperately needed with a few of my friends. Thankfully, they were just as tired of my drinking as I was—maybe even more so. I do not remember exactly what I said or did, but I do recall a friend firmly expressing, "Ok, that is it. It's time." She picked me up (literally—remember, I was scrawny), threw me over her shoulder, and carried me to the car. She dropped me off at Mercy Horizons.

After waking up so many times during my active alcoholism in foreign places—different cities from where I remembered being, unknown residences, and even ICU units —I once again was somewhere I didn't want to be. So what happened when I woke up? I was hung-over and riddled with fear. I started screaming at the nurses. It was all I knew to do.

"I had a solid GPA in college! I am wearing a polo shirt, people! Let me out of here! Don't you know who I am? I don't belong here!"

The God who loves me more than I will ever understand sent another angel into my life. Linda, a recovery counselor, came into the room and sat on my bed.

"Most of what you just said I am sure is true," she said gently. "I am sure you did well in college, and yes, you are wearing a cute polo shirt." She continued, "But I am not so sure you know who you are. What I do know about you is that you have covered your emotions with alcohol for a long time. Isn't that right?"

Her gentle words pacified me. "Well, yes," I supposed. "Yes, that is a fair assumption."

Linda stood up and started to walk out of my hospital room. She turned around when she reached the door and asked a question I later realized was actually a statement. She wanted to give me the perception I had some control.

"Why don't you stay here a few days and see if you can learn a little more about who you really are and maybe determine if we can help you figure out where you belong."

As she left, I secretly acknowledged I didn't like the person I was or respect the way I was living. This time would finally prove to be different. Because of the Holy Spirit and a compassionate angel named Linda, this time would be the last time I would ever awake in that much destructive emotional pain. It would be the last time awaking at a new setting at which I couldn't recall arriving.

I knew alcohol wasn't working for me anymore. I knew there was a God. Concerned families had taken me to church since I was a teenager. In that room, I thought of the Smith Family and how they had done an intervention for me when I was fifteen. They had an active AA member take me to a meeting afterwards. So many people had told me I was worth more than the pain that comes from each drunk. Finally, in that moment in that hospital bed, I was flooded with all the many voices of love. For the first time, these voices were louder than the voices of shame.

On that very day in a hospital room, I tearfully shouted out the cry of surrender. *God help me!* He had been there all along, but on this day, I was finally willing to see His hand on my life. I was finally able to understand the journey was not mine alone. It would be a road where I ultimately learned about the power of emotion—particularly shame—and discovered where I belong and to Whom.

So began my road to sobriety.

CHAPTER 11

THERAPY

The difference between empty and empathy is "AH."
Be someone's AH.

~ KBH

Before I left detox at Mercy Horizons, Linda pleaded with me to choose continued inpatient treatment. I declined since I valued my job and my "vacation" time was expiring. If I'm honest, I also believed I would likely drink again and didn't want to waste the time or effort. We agreed on a plan that would instead have me participate in an intensive outpatient program.

On the first night of group therapy, I walked in with an attitude larger than our local mega church. As I sat among the group, I sized everyone up, which means I compared myself—as I always did. Notice I didn't say *I sat in the group*. I quickly determined every conceivable reason why I did not—should not—belong with "these people." Each person introduced himself and herself, as is customary in any group setting. One woman, Tracey, explained that she was there as part of a job interview. She thanked all of us for allowing her to attend and stated she would simply be observing. My attitude soured even more.

After introductions, the group counselors, Christine and Kelly, tried desperately to help us understand why attending AA meetings, acquiring sponsors, and working the Twelve Steps were vital to sobriety. Since my first AA meeting at the age of fifteen, I could not comprehend why sitting around and talking would ever arrest my daily drinking. It just never made sense. It didn't make sense on this occasion either.

Obviously I wasn't the only one with this reservation since most of the other group members were chiming in with similar complaints and questions. That's when interviewee Tracey, at a full five feet and two inches tall, stood up and asked in her best Pittsburghese (she was from Pittsburgh, Pennsylvania), "Can I show yinz something?"

The counselors very happily agreed since they realized they were not making any progress with this ragtag bunch of misfits. Tracey invited another woman, Mary who was a participant in the group, to stand up and proclaimed, "You will be you."

Simple enough. Then she asked a man—we'll call him Gary— to join Mary; Tracey had him represent alcoholism/addiction and directed him to make sure Mary could not get away. She placed Gary behind Mary and encouraged her, "Okay, Mary your alcoholism is standing right behind you! Try to get away."

Mary thought for a second then took a step forward. When she did, Gary grabbed Mary's arm. Tracey turned and looked at all of us.

"Her disease is too close to her, right?"

We all nodded our heads.

"Mary needs some help. Kim will you stand up and be AA meetings?"

I agreed and took my place. "Now you, Claire, be a sponsor." Tracey pointed to another woman in the group.

Claire tucked herself in behind me. Tracey continued, "And you, Sally, you can represent working the Twelve Steps."

Sally joined us. Tracey said to all of us, "Your job is to protect Mary. Gary your job is to lure her back in."

All of us took the job of safeguarding Mary from Gary very seriously. After scurrying around and engaging in more laughter than any of us had experienced in awhile, Tracey spoke up again, "This is why you need to go to meetings and follow protocols. It creates distance between you and your addiction."

Standing there, it all hit me. For the first time, I got it. I completely understood why I had to follow directions if I wanted to get better. For the previous decade, I had been haphazardly following AA protocol with great resistance, rebelling as my nature led. That night, I surrendered to the full measure of solutions people had been attempting to get me to try for years.

Soon after Tracey's job interview, the one that helped me change my outlook on protocols, alcoholism, and sobriety, the outpatient treatment center that had influenced me so much let us all know they were closing down the facility.

In the natural world, it doesn't make any sense why a failing corporation would have someone in for an interview. In the supernatural world, I understand it. In fact, I'm grateful for it. I understand that God loves me so much that He would orchestrate for Tracey to come into that session on that evening to show me the path on which He wanted me. I firmly believe He loves you that much, too.

Through His loving mercy, God helped me understand:

Alcoholism is similar to being in elementary school where everyone has a friend. We are grouped together–giggling about inside jokes and hugging each other –all while we sit in the sterile hallway with our heads between our knees, preparing for an incoming tornado. Alcoholism is staring at our white converse shoes, noticing the right shoelace is untied and not having the energy to reach down and fix it. When alcohol entered my life, not only did I gain that best friend who hugged me and tied my shoe for me, I also acquired the attention of those who already had friends. Drinking was my golden ticket to fitting in and gave me a (pseudo) sense of belonging. While it is true that alcohol became the tornado, the fact is, in the beginning it was my everything. Today I know that unless God is my every thing, then everything is nothing. So now, nothing feels like everything.

I started attending many more AA meetings. I couldn't get enough. One night, I went to one of these various meetings, and what do you know—Tracey was standing there! We started talking, and well we ended up talking for years. She became one of my best friends for a long season. When we used to hang out, she would never let me forget that it was partly her brilliance that got me to where I am today.

At the same meeting where I reconnected with Tracey, I met my sponsor for my early sobriety. While working the Twelve Steps alongside this sponsor, accepting her guidance, and continuing therapy, I decided I wanted to stand up and help others as much as I felt people were standing up to help me.

CHAPTER 12

ADVANCED THERAPY

When we uncover what we have covered, then we recover.

~ KBH

Can we back track for a moment? When you're gifted with Attention-Deficit-Hyperactivity-Disorder—which by the way is not a disorder but a blessorder—sometimes moving in the opposite direction is the way to go. In truth, it's safe to say that any direction is a way to go.

As a child, my mother always took me to meet with very elite, pretentious therapists who were nothing short of clones of her (not that that is even possible). Mitzi Winesett had been the opposite. She was down-to-earth and embodied the antithesis of my past childhood experiences.

One year before I was sober, I started seeing a new therapist. Her name was Ruthie Epting. My experience with Mitzi during my college years had softened my attitude toward therapy, but I was still leery. Once the outpatient center closed down, my weekly visits for continuing care ended. I wanted to quit. I figured I knew enough and could manage on my own. Everyone around me knew this was a lie. In fact, it's the quintessential "addict's lie:" *I can do this on my own.* No one would let me quit; the team loved me too much. I'm grateful now for their persistence, as it ended up changing my life forever. In order to gain further support, I contacted Ruthie and resumed therapy with her. I wanted—needed—someone familiar.

Ruthie was a very special, albeit unusual, kind of therapist. I was pleased to discover that she was in a world of her own. Unique. Genuine. *Authentic.* Ruthie used to sit on the floor and do her nails while I talked to her. She brought her dogs to the office so at any point, Ruthie or myself could be mid-sentence when one of her dogs would French kiss the open mouth of whomever was speaking. The sloppy kisses and nail painting were refreshing to my soul, the one that still harbored daily thoughts of not being good enough. Her authenticity allowed me to be free, live as myself, and share all about my deep-seated thoughts and feelings.

Some of those feelings included ones exposed after a falling out with my friends from AA. These friends had become my everything. However, many of the friendships had been built through the foundation of control. They knew that in my emotional fragility as a newly recovering addict, they could manipulate me. As I became healthier, I became well enough to say, "Stop!" to those where were trying to control me. The relationships ended abruptly; I was distraught. These had been my "friends"—ones whom I thought were supporting me. Thankfully, I had an appointment that very day with Ruthie. I remember being tremendously emotional in her office—beyond upset.

Ruthie sat me down and started to draw on a piece of paper. She drew a triangle cut into thirds laterally with horizontal lines. In the bottom section of the triangle, she wrote "Acquaintances." In the middle third, she wrote "Good Friends," and in the top section she wrote "Best Friends." I'll never forget the lesson Ruthie taught me that day. Most people in the world fall into the bottom third of our triangles—acquaintances. She explained that some of my friends from AA might have been in that category. Some may have even been in the "Good Friends" section. Then, she asked me to name some people that fell into my top third. This exercise helped me put things into perspective. I still had good friends and best friends who were in my life, ready and willing to support me. I stopped crying and immediately understood, *I'm okay!*

One day Ruthie made a recommendation that changed the direction of my life completely. She supposed, "You know...you might want to think about going to the University of South Carolina and getting your MSW (Master of Social Work). That is what I did, and I think it would work out for you, too."

"Hmmm. That might not be a bad idea. I will check into that."

"Good," said Ruthie as her dog's tongue zeroed in on her mouth.

I started the application process, and to my surprise several months later, I received an acceptance letter from the University of South Carolina (USC). As you may remember, USC is the school I had always wanted to attend. That acceptance letter meant more to me than anyone probably realized, including myself.

Conversation with My Mother:

Kim: "Mother, what did you say yesterday that was so funny?"

Mother: "I don't know. I do know we were discussing what to buy me for Christmas, and you offered to get me a one way ticket to Panama."

Kim: "Yes! Now I remember."

> Mother: "Along with that one way ticket, I want new luggage and a VCR."
>
> Kim: "Mother, please don't say VCR. It is a DVD or Blu-Ray."
>
> Mother: "Well, I want to tell you something, but I am afraid you will tell everyone."
>
> Kim: "I have nothing but secrets in my head, Mother. I am a therapist."
>
> Mother: "I am not telling you. You were a difficult child, and you are even more difficult now. As a matter of fact, you are the most difficult child to ever live."
>
> Kim: "Do I win something for that? A trophy or cash!?"
>
> [She giggles.]
>
> Mother: "Just get some cash and buy me a VCR."
>
> Kim: "MOTHER! STOP SAYING VCR! IT IS 2017! You have a Blu-Ray downstairs. Go watch it."
>
> Mother: "I have to go but you are a very difficult child."
>
> Kim: "So I have been told."

I cherished the acceptance letter and safely tucked it away. It would not become the next casualty of my mother's tactics. You see, that very first acceptance letter to the law school in Michigan was not the only important piece of mail that had disappeared.

One of the few times I visited home while in college, I received a letter of congratulations from a member of the House of Representatives for my college accomplishments. (I tried to tell you I attended classes and was successful despite my drinking habits!)

I came in through the front door and cautiously swerved to the right to acknowledge my mother in the kitchen. After exchanging compulsory greetings, she told me I had some mail. I read the letter as I stood in my mother's beautiful kitchen. I smiled with the feelings one acquires from being recognized, and then I set it on the island countertop before I grabbed my bags and headed for my bedroom. After I unpacked, I went back into the kitchen to talk to my mom. As I walked in, I noticed the island was completely clear.

"Mom, I put my letter right there," I said as I pointed to the exact spot on the island.

"I threw it away. That is what you get for not putting it in its proper place."

I had learned a valuable lesson from that experience. This time around, I kept the USC acceptance letter safe in my hands. It was from USC; it was my top school of choice, and no one was going to throw it away.

I soon discovered I could not maintain my position as a probation agent and fulfill the MSW program requirements. Only the part-time program allowed students to work. I made the decision to surrender my badge and gun in exchange for a new backpack and some heavy textbooks.

CHAPTER 13

A RELENTLESS PURSUIT

"You think outside the box."
"Why wouldn't I? It's not my box," I replied.

~ KBH

As I've described through the telling of my story in the first half of this book, I was never a slacker. Since before my conception, God created me to be relentless. For the first couple decades of my life, I relentlessly pursued the wrong things. I was never lazy. God designed me to be resourceful, persistent, and energetic—in all things. I had no inkling He would use that for His Kingdom later.

Conversation with Mother:

Mother: "Hello."
Kim: "Mom! I got in! I made it! I am a TEDx speaker!"
Mother: "That is wonderful."
Kim: "Tell Daddy, please."

> *Mother: (Completely different tone) "Tell him your own self."*
> *Kim: "Mother, isn't he sitting right beside you?"*
> *Mother: "No. He is outside grilling out."*
> *Kim: Well, okay then. Gotta go tell the world. Bye, Mother!"*

I have always been intrinsically motivated to run. In fact, I'm fairly certain I was born feet first in order to come out running. I ran before my drinking ever became heavy. I ran from my pain. I ran to maintain my weight. I ran because I enjoyed it. I ran in every sense of the word. I love the challenge of running longer distances, which in my case is upwards of seven to ten miles. I've completed six half-marathons.

When I was younger, though, something always held me back from truly excelling at running. It was nothing in the physical sense. In 7th Grade, it was the issue of my birth certificate. My parents couldn't find it in time, so I couldn't compete. In 8th Grade, I had become a full-fledged alcoholic and drug user. I was eventually caught with "speed" at school. Ironic, huh? The school did what was required, and I was kicked off the track team. In 11th Grade, I started running again with the hope that it would replace my drinking. It didn't. I had to drop from the team when I entered the inpatient treatment center. When I returned, I showed up to every track meet intoxicated. That was the end of that.

Fast-forward many years. When I was in treatment for my eating disorders in 2006, I started running again, and it gave me the motivation to start eating again. Today, I run because it's more time to spend with the God who loves me and created me to run. I run to enjoy the body I still get to use here on earth ... the one that had been broken in a hospital bed with no expectations of being able to walk again. I run to praise His Name, to give thanks that I have a life to live for Jesus.

God designed me with the understanding that doing my best at whatever it is I'm doing is the only way to live not just a satisfying life, but ideally, an abundant life. I did everything in a way that honored my personality. My "well" wasn't someone else's "well," and strangely, I was content with that. In hindsight, it was (and is!) a true gift—the ability to honor yourself and your own best in everything you do.

In my pain, I pursued the objects of my addictions. In my sobriety, I learned to pursue health, stability, and an advanced education that would lead me to a profession I now love to wake up to each day. I also learned about the need for belonging and connecting, which motivates me to develop relationships and cooperate with others. Without understanding this innate need we all have for community, I would only strive to be independent and successful in my sobriety. That's not enough. Believe it or not, sobriety is not the end goal for addicts. If it were, we would all fail. In recovery, I learned the most important thing of all, the truth that has solidified my health, hope, and joy: I learned to pursue the One who loves me unconditionally and saved me from myself. And since that moment of understanding, I have never been alone.

The following is an edited post from my blog, titled "I am Resurrected," published on April 8, 2017:

> On this day, 22 years ago, I was given the opportunity to choose to continue doing what I was doing or to allow rehabilitation to become my resurrection.
>
> Since then, I have explored why alcohol had more purpose than I did at that point. I learned the difference between sobriety and recovery.

I can be sober and not in recovery, but I cannot be in recovery unless I am sober.

In recovery, I learned that I used alcohol to abuse myself enough so that people knew someone had abused me first.

Alcohol mimicked the voices of bullies: the rejection, degradation, and overall shame.

As an ironic result, I've learned that not doing well isn't a threat to living out my sober Godly purpose. Instead, it is achieving my dreams that threaten the stability I began seeking 22 years ago.

As continued speaking requests, compliments, and surprising acknowledgment of my gifts pour in, my once neglected spirit is repaired and repurposed.

Here, however, is the crazy part: receiving exactly what I need wakes up the shameful voice that says, "If things go well for you, no one will know what they did to you."

This cry of shame is strangely the cry for help.

I believe this struggle resonates for many of us. Alcohol and other forms of shame-based behavior served as my voice and my way of showing those who hurt me the depth of my pain.

My battle isn't really against food or alcohol or any addictive substance.

Instead, it is a fight against seeking a hug from the armless; a struggle against dependency on those who hurt me versus the One who hurt for me.

By learning alcohol's purpose in my life, I discovered His purpose for my life.

Today, I choose Him and His purpose for me.

In early sobriety and at certain times it has been crucial that I hyper-focused on life events. I learned to not cover or erase my past but to find purpose in the pain.

I will not act like my pain didn't and doesn't exist, nor do I ever want to be so engulfed in my own personal pain that I can't hurt for people in Syria.

Alcohol no longer has purpose in my life but my pain does. Today, when I choose Him, I choose me.

With 22 years sobriety, God and I will go for a run, work on upcoming talks, continue to write my book, meet with my pastor, go to a church event, and most of all, remember my pain and the pain He went through for me.

Long before I was rejected and abused, Jesus was rejected, beaten, and crucified.

On the third day, He was resurrected. Every day, for the last 22 years, has been the third day for me.

I am resurrected.

Steps eight and nine of the Twelve Steps discuss making amends with people whom we have harmed. The Twelfth Step talks about the spiritual awakening that happens as a result of walking those first eleven steps. Someone once explained to me that working through the Twelve Steps is like having a "burning bush" moment, just as Moses did with the Lord. It was described to me (not by any biblical scholar, so don't go checking the Scriptures for this exact storyline; it is not there) that the fire did not consume or burn up the bush because God wanted to open Moses's spiritual eyes. God didn't want Moses to be consumed by his past mistakes, his past sins. Rather, He wanted Moses to be consumed by the fire of God, not wilting or burning up, but on fire with the power and forgiveness of His Spirit. This resonated with me. I longed for a burning bush experience.

In His loving way, God provided. In the earliest season of my spiritual awakening, I ran (pun fully intended here) into an old friend. I was at a print store in Columbia, South Carolina while I was pursuing my Masters Degree. I had tried going to the USC Public Library first, but there was no available parking. I was trying to print a paper, so I took my floppy disk (Google it if you're not sure what I just said) to Kinko's and put it in the motherboard, or whatever it was called back in the day.

While I was messing around with the computer, Jennie, the one whom I had not seen or spoken to since I physically attacked her and tried to destroy everything in one of the rooms of her brand new home, walked in. I knew immediately that God was giving me that burning bush moment. Yet, I was terrified.

I wove my way through the printers right up to Jennie, trembling with the fear of the unknown. *How would she react? How would I feel?*

"Jennie. Hey. Will you talk to me outside?"

She said yes.

When we stepped outside, I explained I didn't remember a whole lot from our last encounter. So she began talking; she needed to recount the entire night. Jennie needed me to know that she had been taken to the hospital. She needed me to know that when her father—who was a very stoic man—walked into her hospital room and saw the bruises and injuries on her face that I had caused, he wept. I faithfully listened to the whole story.

I made amends with Jennie that night. I was able to tell her that I did not get sober that night that I betrayed her trust and assaulted her, "But," I explained to her, "that night keeps me sober." I told her I was living for Jesus.

God knew I would be at Kinko's because He filled up a parking lot. God knew Jennie would be at the same Kinko's because she had frustratingly walked out of her own graduate level class at USC, jumped in her car, discovered her cell phone battery was dead, stopped at a payphone, realized she didn't have a quarter to make a call, and then proceeded to the very Kinko's where I had never planned to be either to get change for a dollar. That is the irrational grace of God!

For so many years, I could see nothing attractive about a loving, good God. My initial bond (to my mother) had been painful and full of rejection, so my inner fear wondered why would I want to risk seeking out a loving God. Then I finally learned that the "Good News" of the Gospel wasn't actually good. I learned how Jesus was horribly mistreated. I learned that even His disciples betrayed and rejected Him. I learned that the pain and suffering He endured on the cross were unbearable, and I learned that God could not even watch Jesus' last moments on the cross. I could relate to all of that new knowledge and understanding. The pain of the Gospel resonated with me. Jesus' pain was so much worse than mine. His rejection was beyond my imagination and so tragic that Jesus had even asked His Father if there was another way. In my own humanity, I could get behind all of that. I realized how relatable Jesus really is. The pain of the Gospel saved me. The Love of our Father transformed me. God showed me the difference between His Love and toxic love.

God's love meets us where we are and inspires us to become who He created us to be. Toxic love sees us where we are and tells us it isn't enough. In fact, toxic love tells us that we aren't enough. While God's love propels us to a higher level of worth, toxic love can only take us in one direction— down. We spiral down into depression, eating disorders, self-harm, alcoholism, pornography, gambling, codependency, people-pleasing, and general self-neglect. Whether our abuser is our boss, parent, spouse, or even our pastor, he or she will always want us to neglect ourselves or change ourselves to appease them. When we are under the cloud of toxic love, the shame within the toxicity will always make us feel compelled to do more because we feel small. God's love will propel us to do more for His Kingdom because we feel significant within His deep love. He didn't send His Son for us to feel or be small. We become small as we are suffocated by our abuser's shame. We become large as we are embraced by His love.

I had to learn the difference between what I deserved and for what I was worthy. I had to surrender any possible logical answer to decide what I deserved in life and the struggle of worth. God showed me that on one special Friday, Jesus took everything I deserved onto the cross. I have accepted this fact. Saturday was the day of His burial. I have spent years working on allowing Saturday to be real for me, to truly bury the effects of my sin and shame and everyone else's sin and shame that were so freely shared with me. One of the most comforting Christian sayings for me is "Sunday's coming!" Friday is what I deserve, but God interceded for me. Saturday is my struggle to bury all the things that stop me from receiving His love. Sunday is the day I walk out via His Love, His resurrection. My worth is as significant as the tomb is empty. My experience with feeling worthy is based on how much I am empty of the sin and shame for which He died. It's no longer about what I deserve. I am worthy in Him.

My spiritual awakening meant that I was now awakened. I had a life-changing and final decision to make. Either I was going to believe God was in charge or I was going to believe He wasn't. I chose to believe He was for me, even when I was against me. I started looking for Him instead of looking for rejection. My spiritual awakening meant I was in agreement with who He said I was and not with my life experiences, my mother, all the invalidating men in my life, or not even just with my daddy. Him. The Almighty said I was worthy of being raised up by and for Him. I was awake and resurrected!

I tell you about this burning bush moment because it was significant, not only because God had orchestrated our meeting after so many years had gone by, but also because I was in a place of agreement with God. I could hear that Jennie had been transported to the hospital that night and not hurt myself in retaliation for the pain I felt. I was able to hurt for Jennie, hurt for my past self, and praise the fact that I was no longer in a place that the shame from my previous choices and addiction could control me. I had surrendered the shame and surrendered my past to the cross.

As a resurrected Daughter of the Almighty, my pursuit of Christ has become relentless. In the most significant aspect of my life—my faith journey—you better believe I'm going to surrender it all. If it's worth doing, it's worth doing to His standards. AA taught me to "live life on life's term." I learned to translate that to "live life on God's terms," and peer approval stopped being my end goal.

It wasn't long before I started looking for Him in everything. It is close to impossible to look and expect His grace and mercy while actively participating in victim mentality. I realized he had always been in my life. I had just never noticed Him because I had not shown up for my own life. It became evident that life went well when I got out of His way. Then I could see His Will for me. When I look back now, I don't know how I missed all the miracles. Well, actually, I do. I was drunk, and I believed I didn't deserve a miracle. But now I was one of the examples mentioned in the Bible—one of His countless children who was blind but who had been given sight.

I could see the miracle of being a patient in a treatment center at age seventeen – one that kicked me out for being too emotionally unstable—and nine years later, becoming the one of the group therapists. I was awakened to see that the detox center I had left AMA (against medical leave) and then returned to for my recovery eventually become where I worked and professionally helped others detox safely. I had the mud removed from my eyes so I could see that it wasn't really me who mistakenly filled in the circle for college

Columbia College instead of USC at the SAT Testing Center. I became aware that He was the one who cared about every hair on my head, so He had orchestrated for one of His other children to write "Psychology" as my major under my name in the college directory. He was the One who lead me to a church, Mosaic in Charlotte, that quite possibly has the only ex-Muslim pastor, a pastor who had heard "no" so many times in his life that he felt compelled to say "yes" to me when I asked to start a mental health ministry in his church. And, I'm positively sure God has his Hand over this new ministry of His (not mine) that led me to meeting Cortney, my ghostwriter. I am getting ahead of myself (for the tenth time), but I want all of you to know that God is active in our lives, and once we know we are worthy of a personal relationship with Him, then we can see and encounter Him with each breath we take.

When I moved to the Charlotte area and opened my own psychotherapy practice, I made it a priority to find a church home where I felt accepted and encouraged. I dove deeply into His Word, and I made the recommitment to continue to live my life according to His plan. After all, my plans through all the years had not really worked out.

I relentlessly pursued God and continued to see how His Hand was all over my life. Also during this time, my friend Tracey, whom I told you about earlier in my recovery story, once again taught me something invaluable. She shared the basic components of Transactional Analysis (TA): wounded child, rebellious teenager, critical parent, and adult self. TA was another way I was able to understand why I felt so fragmented. That critical parent voice, the voice of shame, wasn't allowed to be my parent anymore.

One beautiful and sunny April morning, I readied myself for a run. If you know me, you are aware that this is a normal Saturday morning routine for me. I love going with my running partner. On this particular day, she was on vacation with her husband and four grown children.

For ten years, I have run the same path. It takes us from my house to the end of the neighborhood in the gigantic residential development I affectionately call "the hood." The entire loop is a 5K (3.2 miles). Typically, runners use Saturdays as their longer run days. Since my running partner was out of town, I decided not to travel somewhere like a greenway or uptown Charlotte to run alone. I still wanted to go a longer distance, so I stepped out of my house, took a deep breath, and consciously decided to not do what I had always done (please read into this).

Once I reached the main road, I turned left instead of right onto the parkway to head the opposite direction through the hood. I had no idea God was really the One who had made that decision through the prompting of the Holy Spirit within me.

As I ran, I became uniquely aware of how many cars were flying past me. I wondered if they realized that the hill they were so aggressively going up was even a hill. I was curious if the drivers of the cars knew that as we all went downhill, they were aware of the danger of gravity. Probably not. Gravity was potentially dangerous for me as a runner, not so much for them as they sat protected by their car.

When I run downhill, I lean forward a little which results in an increase of my speed. I should probably wear a fall risk bracelet (you know the one you get at the hospital). I pay attention to every uneven part of the sidewalk, curb, and tree branch as I run. Those who are driving most likely won't wreck over a twig, but I could. What is my point?

My point is that even when we are on the same path, we all have different circumstances, perspectives, and vehicles on that path. Many of you had mothers that were as powerful as Porsches in how they were able to affectively minister to your needs. Others had a "Honda mom," very reliable and long lasting. But for some of us, our caregivers resembled broken-down mopeds, pawnshop bikes, or perhaps we only had our own two feet as our modes of transportation.

Also on this April day as I ran, learning from God this enlightening message about perspective, a woman (whom I had never met) came up running alongside me. We exchanged pleasantries. Then she looked me in the eyes and claimed, "You are my pacesetter."

We were running up a hill at that moment. (It turned out the new path I chose that morning was nothing but humongous hills.) The profound meaning of what she said hit me like road kill.

Yes, I am so glad that many of you had a secure attachment with your mom. You had a more-than-good-enough mom. She made you feel accepted, chosen, and cherished whether you were running uphill or not. You knew you were safe with her driving your life, and in time, you were excited to then have her as your passenger and friend. I am grateful some of you knew your moms absolutely, unconditionally loved you. This book is for you, too. However, someone who walked alone, up all the hills, and with no earthly pacesetter wrote this book.

When that woman looked me square in the sunglasses and said I was her pacesetter, God showed me that it was not *in spite* of me being on a different path, but *because I was on a different path* that I was a unique pacesetter. This feels almost egotistical to say. Perhaps it's because my mother still tells me all the time that I have an EGO. (Though, most of the time she misuses the word.) On that run not too long ago, God impressed upon my heart that I was chosen to set the pace for those of us who didn't have a Honda, Lexus, or Toyota mother.

On that spring morning, I ran the exact distance I would have if I had turned right instead of left, but it was a more difficult path. The hills were unforgiving, yet it was in the grueling rises where I met my one true Pace Setter. If I had turned right and run the same perpetual path, I would never have learned that my different path was my divine path. The different and difficult path may be your divine path as well.

Life was going well. I was becoming more obedient to God's design for my life with each passing year. I continued to call my parents and check in. I was fully in their lives, but I was still reeling with every interaction with my mother. I was surprised my mother showed interest in the ministry I founded – icuTalks. Something about it made sense to her, but what she couldn't quite understand was that it was a ministry. She (still) calls it a missionary. So when in Rome—or Panama, in this case—we all adapt and say what Mother says. The volunteers now call it a missionary. For those of you who are interested, it is a speaking mental health ministry (missionary) and more information can be found at www.icuTalks.com.

Then the day came that we all eventually experience as Christ-followers—the day the Lord requires us to die to our ideas of self-preservation in order to be obedient to Him. You see, in recovery, I had died to my old self in order to save my physical self. Sobriety finally came and stayed, and it was for my sole (and soul) benefit. Yet, God wanted me to live the abundant spiritual life as well, not just the safe one. I was going to have to pick up my own cross daily, and put Him and His desires first. This time, it had nothing to do with my sobriety.

The day I first felt Jesus prompting me to fully reconcile with my mother, give her the level of grace He had offered me, and relentlessly pursue forgiveness for decades of wrong-doing, is a day I'll never forget.

CHAPTER 14

THE CHOICE

Shame is the enemy's weapon of choice because in its grip, we not only forget we have choices, we also forget Who chose us.

~ KBH

Even though I am a psychotherapist and have the credentials to diagnosis my patients, I don't like placing labels on people. Maybe that is a result of having a plethora of diagnoses hovering over me. Starting at the age of seven, I have been diagnosed with bipolar disorder, anorexia, bulimia, oppositional defiant disorder, ADHD, PTSD, and alcohol dependence. (Okay, I will give them that one!) While I never want my patients or anyone else to believe they are their psychiatric labels, I do believe the diagnoses are part of the roadmap to healing.

I am not going to diagnose my mother with anything she hasn't been diagnosed with from other health care professionals. She, just like me, has one label worthy of mentioning, and that is *God's Daughter*. Therefore, I am just going to provide the criteria for two types of narcissism. You can do what you choose with this information.

There are many professionals in the mental health field who believe that narcissistic personality disorder is severe PTSD that morphs into a personality disorder. The two types of narcissists relevant to this conversation are malignant and vulnerable. I can say with certainty that you know a handful of malignant narcissists. They are the stereotypical heterosexual, Caucasian, successful CEO-type men. They not only lack empathy, they laugh at it. They deflect everything and use their callous personalities to make business and family decisions in a way that some people might admire. There may even be at least one man coming to mind for you right now. Ahem. Moving on people!

What is not discussed enough in our society is the vulnerable narcissist. While both types of narcissism have many characteristics in common (disdain towards almost everyone, lack of awareness of their impact on others, refusal to be inconvenienced, and being self-consumed), the vulnerable narcissist is more difficult to detect. These individuals cause death of self and destroy relationships with others by a thousand paper cuts rather than a handful of swift and fierce relational knife wounds.

Vulnerable narcissists are more emotionally sensitive. They struggle with abandonment and bobble between inferiority and superiority. They tend to feel victimized when not treated the way they expect but can also regress if they receive too much attention. Vulnerable narcissists are preoccupied with fears of rejection and abandonment and place responsibility of how they feel on others. More than likely, the vulnerable narcissistic mother or father was raised by a disorganized parent and never learned how to regulate levels of safety or closeness. They had constant messaging from a caregiver that roared, "Come here; go away!"

I called my mother countless times to ask if I could drop by and see her. Ninety percent of those times, her response was *no*. She explained it would cause her too much stress to be around me. When you have a vulnerable narcissistic mother, it is common to embrace the rejection and wrap it into your identity. I minimized what she did to me and believed how I was feeling was my fault. It created an internal struggle. When I expressed my confusion about this with others, they would inevitably say (you know where I am going), "But she loves you." I cannot express how hard it was to sift through the pain and discover what was mine to own and what truly belonged to her.

Conversation with My Mother:

Kim: "Hey, Mother."

Mother: "Mother's Day is coming up."

Kim: "Yes, Ma'am. I know. What is the plan?"

Mother: "I guess we can go to a restaurant."

Kim: "Which one, Mother?"

Mother: "Well I don't know since you both live so far away." (She is referring to Jimmy Jimmy Jimmy and me.)

Kim: "Mother, I have always lived far away and have always traveled to see you on Mother's Day. The difference is your son just moved far away from you."

[Long pause.]

Mother: "Well, I love Jimmy more than I love you."

Kim: "Thank you, Mother. Just wanted you to say it. Don't you feel better now that you spoke your truth?"

Mother: "You are ridiculous."

Kim: "You are ridiculous."

Mother: "You are!"

Kim: "You."

Mother: "No, your father is ridiculous!"

You have just experienced a sane moment in the life of insanity...

In my early thirties, my brother, his family, and I went to my parents' residence to celebrate the Fourth of July. After a fun time in the pool with my brother's phenomenal children, we all dried off and went inside. We gathered around in my parents' living room to talk. Please know—talking for us doesn't mean trading life updates, work situations, praises, or complaints. No way. We mainly construct witty comments to share and then stare at each other during the silences. People don't believe me, but this truly is our family time. No one asks about each other. Individually, we do share some news with each other, but corporately it just isn't our way.

Anyway, my mother announced she had a gift for everyone. *Jackpot!* My parents are very generous people. My mother handed my father a gift, and he opened it. She handed Jimmy Jimmy Jimmy a gift, and he opened it. She handed a gift to his (then) wife, followed by each of their children. Everyone sat with a brand new gift in his or her lap. Well, everyone but me. I had learned by now to have a little bit of a voice.

"Um, Mom. Um, well ... what about me?"

"I didn't know what to get you," she justified.

"So you got me nothing?"

Mother replied, "That's right."

I lost my voice at that point. (For future reference, cash is always a great gift for me.)

When you have a mother who intentionally doesn't give you a gift, tells you not to call home, and expresses that you are too stressful to be around (all while others continue to articulate that is love), then ALL relationships become difficult.

Years passed by and my faith grew. For quite some time, I had been so focused on sobriety. My goal had been *I won't drink in this second.* Then, I moved to the next second and made the self-promise again. The moment I surrendered to Jesus in that hospital bed, I became a Christian. But, it took years for my internal transformation to significantly affect my feelings and actions. I think every Christian probably goes through a faith journey similar to mine. My surrender was huge because it was the sincere realization and an intentional admission that I needed a Savior, but it was also tiny in retrospect. Over time, the genuine emotions and willful surrender came, and life began to change. I began to change.

One day in the not-so-distant past, I called my mother. As soon as I started to say *hello,* she interrupted me.

"I don't want to talk to you right now."

The echoes of rejection from my first phone call from college to home rang in my heart. The feelings of not being good enough for gifts, compliments, praises, or connection leapt to the forefront of my soul.

For decades, I had struggled with too much shame to think my needs mattered. Yet at this point in my life, I knew that I mattered because I knew my Savior, and He told me I was fearfully and wonderfully made. I am His daughter. Precious and beloved.

I hung up the phone. This was my internal monologue:

"That's it! I know about boundaries. I teach others about boundaries. I don't want to keep doing this!" Her telling me she didn't want to talk to me had been a common occurrence my whole life. On this day, with this particular call, I had finally hit my breaking point.

Then, God came near and my pain-filled monologue became an intimate dialogue.

Kim, I want you to pursue this relationship.

I heard Him clearly, and I thought for a moment He was disoriented. God must be confused. I know He isn't a God of confusion, but how in the world could I reconcile with someone to whom I had never measured up? Then I remembered the mantra I had learned throughout my recovery: *Live life according to God's terms.*

"God! Did you not see and hear what just happened? It's not like this was the first time! You've watched her reject me my whole life!"

Fill yourself up with Me, and then call her. Every day.

I didn't want to, but I relented. I had come so far in understanding that God's way was always the best way. I knew I could trust His promises and His love for me. I started to pray. I filled myself with His Spirit, and I called my mother every day.

In the beginning, it was a cup-full of difficult. My mother would answer the phone with, "Whaaaat do you want?" or "Don't talk to me." There was bilateral bitterness injected into nearly every conversation. Yet, I persisted in my prayers, and He gave me a cup-and-a-half measure of patience.

After a particularly difficult and tense conversation, I hung up and said, "God, I can't handle the rejection. I need to have boundaries." I gave myself permission to hang up after ten minutes or three insults, whichever came first. The next several phone calls ended before the ten-minute mark.

Soon after, God orchestrated a turning point. While talking to my dad one day, he indicated, "I want you to know that your mother looks forward to those phone calls every day."

My heart quivered with genuine surprise.

My dad taught me a few truths growing up that have served me more than I could have imagined over the years. One of those truths is *people who truly have power do not have to show it. People who are in control do not have to prove they are in control.* In my conversations with my mother, I was reminded of my dad's wisdom. I am very grateful for my dad and even more grateful for my Heavenly Father.

Our conversations after that had a different tone. She seemed slightly kinder. I was able to hang up without needing to shred many feelings of shame or rejection. I kept looking to God for strength, patience, and grace. In fact, I learned how to stop looking to the one who hurt me and instead look to the One who hurt *for* me.

The shift was slow but steady. My mother and I began to have more candid conversations. Humor and wit etched themselves into the flow of our daily chats. Best of all, I noticed she no longer spoke about Jimmy Jimmy Jimmy all the time. Notice, I wrote *all the time.* Yes, she still talked about him, and there was an elevated excitement in her voice when she said his name. Yet in those moments, I chose to remind myself of how God's voice sounded when He said my name—filled with delight and dipped in perfect love. This knowledge satisfied my soul.

Choices. Adults have choices. In those moments when I *feel* like I don't have a choice, I am emotionally regressed. John Lee, the man who founded P.E.E.R. (Primary Emotional Energy Recovery) Therapy and from whom I learned so much, taught me that emotional regression is when I move from acting like a clear-thinking and feeling adult to having the limited thoughts and strategies of a child.

Prior to calling her each time, it was imperative that I made sure I was an adult, that my God-self was the one driving the call and reacting to her words. It was my responsibility to know what would trigger me into an emotional regression or a trauma state. A large segment of my recovery was focusing on my responsibility, my need, and to no longer have someone else in charge of how I felt or perceived myself. To put it in AA terms, it is all about "being current." My responsibility was to build my emotional sobriety to a point that my response to a situation wasn't disproportionate to reality, to not be over or underwhelmed.

Robert D. Stolorow is a psychoanalyst and philosopher known for his works on intersubjectivity theory, post-Cartesian psychoanalysis, and emotional trauma. He is also the author of one of my favorite quotes: "As children, we must find a way to organize the profusion of stimuli with which we are confronted. Strongly influenced by our parents and teachers and by earlier events in our lives, we form unconscious principles to organize current stimuli. Since these principles operate outside our awareness, it seems to us we are merely responding to the reality of any given situation. When those principles don't serve us well in later years, we go into therapy to bring them into consciousness, weaken their hold on us, and give us new choices."

I made a conscious choice to acknowledge I was in a strong hold, and to break free from it, I had to stop believing the thoughts I had believed for the longest in order to learn about the One who had been pursuing me the longest. I chose to continue this practice every day. I filled myself with truth and love, seeking the Holy Spirit, and then I called Mother. God has already provided people in my life who could (and will continue to) meet my needs. I know they are human, so when they don't meet my needs, He is there to fill in all the gaps when I seek His face.

I chose to let my mother be exactly where she was, and I focused instead on where I was. I stopped blaming and neglecting myself. I made a conscious choice that her neglectful and abusive ways of treating me would no longer be acceptable. I chose to let what happened next work for me. I made the decision for my expectations and history with her to be congruent. I made a conscious choice to no longer have the possibility of my mother's approval be more important than me getting hurt. I looked at her through adult lenses, not those of my wounded inner little girl. I chose to be creative with my strategies. I did not allow her possible and predictable reaction to be more of a relevant factor than me having a voice. And I no longer waited for an apology from her; instead, I let my newfound behavior be an apology from me to me. I chose to be authentically imperfect.

And, everything changed.

In fact, just the other day, I jokingly asked her, "Mother, how are you not locked up? If you weren't beautiful, you'd be in an institution." My mother was able to agree and laugh alongside me. Light-hearted. Truth encased in love. Because of all my healing —my choices—this is the place we find ourselves now.

Many of you might be thinking *I would never speak to my mother that way*. And, many of you are correct. You wouldn't. My mother and I had to find our own language. It is ours and works for us. Without me being open to finding our own authentic balance of love and truth, I would not have any kind of relationship with her, much less the beautiful one I have with her today.

Conversation with My Mother:

Kim: "Hey, Mother."

Mother: (in a flat tone/affect) "Hi."

Kim: "What's wrong, Mother?"

Mother: "Nothing. I am just tired from working in the yard yesterday."

Kim: "Oh, okay. Well, pray for "missionary" tonight, please." *(If you remember, her use of the term missionary refers to the icuTalks ministry I founded.)*

Mother: "I need you to pray for me. I was in the garden yesterday praying about all my bad thoughts."

Kim: (Giggling) "What kind of thoughts?"

Mother: Just people like our yard guy, but I was also thinking about all the challenges in our lives. I was praying for Jimmy Jimmy Jimmy and his challenges. Then I thought, I wonder what challenges led Kim to God?"

Kim: "MOM!" You thought of me!!! You went from Jimmy to me!!!"

Mother: "Stop it. What challenges got you to church?"

Kim: "What do you think was my challenge?"

Mother: "Life, and you drank a lot, and you were a spoiled brat. You are still a spoiled brat."

[Beautiful laughter at this point.]

Mother: "My challenge is living in Fort Mill. I don't know what Dad's challenge is."

Kim: "You, Mom! You are Dad's biggest challenge. Let us not mince words or waste any time. It is clearly you."

CHAPTER 15

THE 3 R'S

God can't maximize what you minimize.
By placing light on what we don't want to see, clarity comes.
Your whole story matters.

~ KBH

Resiliency has become a commonplace word, but I am not sure many of us have granted ourselves permission to believe that it is a personal, powerful force within us. Resiliency is like our relationship with Jesus. Much like boundaries without action, if my relationship with Jesus isn't personal then it is just an idea, not a practice. I believe how much I pursue Him, which includes removing the barriers that prevent me from personally experiencing Him, is directly proportional to how much I personalize others' comments and actions.

Webster and his friends define resiliency as "the capacity to recover quickly from difficulties; toughness." I'll agree with the toughness part. One needs a measure of grit to be resilient. However, I believe resiliency doesn't necessarily require a quick recovery. I do think to be called *resilient* one must come back stronger and wiser. To be stronger and wiser, we must be cognizant of where his or her feet are currently treading. In resiliency, we acknowledge we are in our own processes. It doesn't have to look like anyone else's path.

I define resiliency as the ability to have a new vision of how to use what has happened to you and learning to live that vision out. Resiliency is about healing. It's about sharing. You've become resilient when you can allow your story to transcend your own perspectives, exit your own little part of the world, and permit it to be useful to others. I have learned to share my story without it being only about me but about how it could serve others. Resiliency is important for our well-being. I want to explain what I believe are the two steps to gaining this full healing and the life of abundance that Jesus wants for us.

The first step is repair. After a singular crisis or a traumatic season, we all must make the choice to move forward. Repairing is moving forward differently. Those who get stuck in the mentality of wanting change but not changing anything are not able to repair.

For me, moving forward differently happened during at least two distinct "aha moments." The first was when I came to the foot of the cross and surrendered my life to Jesus in that hospital bed. That was certainly a "moving forward differently" kind of decision! I had tried for years to establish sobriety on my own, and it never worked. It was when I abandoned my pride, trusted God, and surrounded myself with people who cared deeply, had the necessary professional wisdom, and wholly supported me that things began to change. I changed.

The second "aha moment" that helped me repair was the moment I chose obedience to God in pursuing a relationship with my mother. I began moving forward by setting boundaries, engaging with God through prayer, and filling myself with His Spirit in order to get past the past. I was open to doing something different in how we interacted and how I managed her insults and rejection. My mother was not the one who changed first. I did the grueling training. I directed my steps left when I had normally skidded to the right. I did the dirty internal work, and I focused on where I was and not where she was (or was not). I did something she had struggled to do—I let it be about me. It was the renewed me. I had been victimized but I repaired and became resilient, refusing to live out a victim's story for the rest of my life.

Conversation with My Mother:

Mother: "Kim, I have to ask you something that has bothered me for almost a year."

[I take a deep breath since my mother and I have had hard conversations since she watched my videos about the abuse.]

Kim: "Sure, go ahead."

Mother: "Remember last June when you were following us to the Ballantyne Resort for Father's Day? There was a white car in front of you. The car was going very slowly. Why didn't you pass it?"

Kim: "So...not to minimize or invalidate your question, can you tell me why that would bother you for months?"

Mother: "Because I would have passed it. I don't know. I guess it is my EGO."

Kim: "Mother, I think our time might be better spent discussing the psychological meaning of EGO and helping you with that."

The second step to resiliency is repurposing. To repurpose is to use the thing that was being held against you (shame, addiction, rejection...fill-in-your-own-blank) in service to others. Repurposing positions our weakness or trauma as a stepping stool to something greater than ourselves.

Recently, I was interviewed as one of "50Thrivers" from around the world for *The Global Resiliency Project* to share my story about overcoming addiction and rejection. The interviewer asked me, "How would you define thriving?"

"Thriving is when pain becomes my b—."

Yes, that's what I said, and I don't regret it. It was a true, in-the-moment definition that simply came to me. Or, there is a chance it may have been inspired by the *cuss a little and love Jesus* t-shirt I had recently seen.

Pain no longer owns me; I own it. I have learned how to turn it around, dump it on its rear end, and use it to step up to a higher position where I can see the good that God can do with it. I am not minimizing my pain. I am accepting it, repairing myself, and repurposing it all.

In 2017, I had the absolute privilege of being a TEDx Charlotte speaker. The subject of my talk was shame, but my message was how to allow shame to be our stepping stool to something greater. When we repurpose, it means we have acquired a new position (and view), which means others can see us. We were not created to live small. I can now stand on my shame-laced stepping stool and reach out help to anyone else who is seeking to learn how to repair and repurpose. (P.S. Please go to YouTube and watch my TEDx talk. Y'all know I would love the attention!)

There is a huge difference between pain and needs, between shame and healthy boundaries. If you are shamed for or ashamed of your needs (as I was), you will go into an addiction. What's a need? A need is a physical, social, emotional, or spiritual requirement to build trust that leads to a secure connection—a relationship. Relationships are built on trust, but the trust is a by-product of our needs being fulfilled. If someone consistently fills my need for acceptance while I fill his or her need for significance, we have formed a relationship. Relationships start and end based on the satisfaction of needs.

We all need to know we matter. We all need to feel some measure of importance. Every one of us needs to be seen and heard, and we need to be validated and loved. Only the enemy wants us to be ashamed of our needs. Our needs allow deeper connections, and the enemy is the only one who wants us to live in isolation.

So many of us confuse neglecting ourselves with denying our old selves, meaning we not only refrain from asking for what we need, we don't even know our needs. We labor intensely towards others needs while resenting the fact that no one is noticing we have needs as well. When I used to suffer silently and wait for you to notice my needs, I was actually wanting you to do for me what I was not even doing for myself. When we neglect our needs, what others think of us and how they treat us can become more important than what God thinks of us. That's self-neglect.

Self-destruction is the abuse, neglect, or mistreatment of one's own needs. Today, I am able to deny my old self, the one that believed all the negative labels others had put on me. It was the self that had to drink in order to mask the pain. Yes, I learned how to stop the cycle of self-destruction. Praise God!

Others of us believe the lie that tells us that our needs make us weak. Just as Jesus modeled for us during His forty days in the desert, I hope we all fight back against lies and temptations with God's Word. 2 Corinthians 12:9 in the New International Version of the Bible says, "My grace is sufficient for you, for my power is made perfect in weakness." That's right. His power is made perfect in our weaknesses. The Scripture goes on to say that we should actually boast about our weaknesses! Do you think having needs is weak?

Do you try to hide your weaknesses? I used to. It's what the enemy wanted me to do: Hide my shame. Hide my insecurities. Hide my eating disorders. Hide my pain. But, we are called to love God with everything, which means we are to surrender all. We must surrender our needs and our weaknesses to Him, allow Him to meet us where we are, and honor His ability and desire to repurpose our pain for His glory. After all, when we neglect what we need, we are neglecting the one He saved!

Recovery is reclaiming our God-given needs and removing the shame from them. It's a slow process. For some people, it means removing the toxic people from their lives. For me, it meant reconciling with Mother. Please hear me out. I am not advising that everyone reconcile with those who plow through their boundaries. I am not recommending you neglect yourself in order to maintain a toxic relationship. This is what God asked *me* to do. He may be asking you to do something different.

I know an amazing woman whose mother suffers from Munchausen syndrome by proxy, which means that her mother intentionally caused sickness in my friend's body so that she (the mother) could receive attention. Well-intentioned people often say to her, "But your mother loves you." Well-intentioned people tell her she should return her mother's phone calls and allow her into her adult life. As a psychotherapist or friend, I would never recommend to someone to go hang out with her rapist and love on them until the person is sorry for violently invading her physical body and soul.

Mothers have availability to the most personal parts of our lives—our hearts, our understanding of self, our initial perceptions of God, and of our senses of worth. Unless you hear from the Lord, please keep your physical, social, spiritual, and emotional selves safe. For those of us who have been abused, it is our responsibility to recover. For those of you who didn't have neglectful parents, you can be part of our recovery by not trying to convince us that we aren't where we know we are.

The year this book was written, my Mother watched my TEDx Charlotte talk online. This prompted her to go back and watch all the talks I had ever done for icuTalks up to that point. She had no idea that I had been speaking all those years. She had always asked me if I talked about her in therapy, to my friends, and on Facebook. I never denied doing so. Suddenly, she was hearing the raw honesty I was sharing about our relationship. I had not been shy in telling my story, talking about my pain, and expressing the rejection I had felt from her in those talks. When I found out she had watched them, it physically hurt me to know she had heard all of that. I knew that no one could hear those stories and not feel violated. Her seeking the videos out and hearing my accounts of her abuse erupted deep pain for her. She dissociated from how she treated me and honestly, she needed to do so.

Her response was interesting. Rather than listen to my stories for general understanding or with an overarching perspective, she picked out a couple specific things I said and targeted them. My mother moved from denial, "Kim, I never told you not to come home for the summer while you were in college," to acceptance that she did say such things. Her acceptance quickly slid into justification: "Kim, I said that because you were on the verge of dropping out of school!"

"Actually, Mother, I loved school, and I wanted to stay during the summer; I signed up for a Badminton class. I was never going to drop out."

I never wanted her to feel pain, but I know I could either place my trust in the resurrection power of Jesus, or I could trust all the voices telling me to rescue her. I could rescue her or allow the true Rescuer to come in and redeem it all.

Calling her after she watched the videos suddenly felt the same as in the beginning of our restoration process. I suppose it was two steps forward and one giant step back. I didn't know what would happen, and I would press deeply into the Holy Spirit before picking up the phone. I had to trust that God allowed her to watch the videos in His timing. I had to trust that the crucifixion she was feeling would lead to a resurrection.

I also had to take care that I not make it about me. I had done my work regarding the abuse. My spiritual job was to be there for her and represent my Heavenly Father's love. I knew she could end the relationship. I also knew I was not going to harm myself no matter what happened. I had repaired and my life had been repurposed. This was about her repair and potential repurpose. It was imperative that I let it be about her and not get in the way.

Some time elapsed, and my mother did end up repairing her wounds. It was a beautiful thing to watch. As of the writing of this book, she still brings it up. She claims I told one-third of the truth. That is classic vulnerable narcissism. She wants me to believe that I made her a victim when I was the victim. I laugh with joy to myself because it no longer has power over me. I don't know what will happen if she reads this book or what is next for her. I do know, ironically, I can't make it about her or me. God is the Director, and only He knows if it will be repurposed. I pray it is.

This truth that I now live by and was able to speak into my mother was never something I could have honestly spoken to her in my childhood. Remember, as a child, I viewed my mother as perfection. Speaking my truth and expressing my needs are part of the boundaries and healthy practices I have put in place to care for myself. I pray you are able to do the same in your own life.

CHAPTER 16

THE B WORD

I do not have the power to change you,
but I have the power to not be changed by you.

~ KBH

Boundaries are the offerings I give to my mother (and all those in my life) that tell her how to navigate a relationship with me. When I have boundaries, I am fighting against shame. I am agreeing with God that I am worthy. I am going against the enemy who tries to tell me that I'm not good enough. In the addictions of my past, I was agreeing with the enemy. I would honor the shame rather than honor the truth.

My boundaries are also a product of my faith. For so long throughout my childhood, I feared telling my mother what I needed because I feared I would hurt her feelings. Probably more accurate a statement would be that I feared I would disappoint her. With boundaries, I'm confirming that my faith in God and the fact that my needs matter to Him are bigger than anyone else's rejection of me.

When people say to me, "I didn't want to tell you (such and such) because I didn't want your feelings to get hurt," I struggle. When we say that to others, we're actually making it about us. We're harming ourselves. In effect, we're saying, "I can't handle rejection, so I didn't tell you because I was afraid of your reaction." Which is more important: Adding value to someone's walk with the Lord through honest—albeit tough—conversations, or ensuring they like you? I'm telling you right now, I would rather you add to my character development and faith journey than like me.

My daddy meant well, but he would often say, "Don't tell your mom (such and such)." He was trying to protect her, but he was stripping her of her ability to formulate her own responses, take ownership of her own emotional health, and build a relationship with her daughter. After awhile, I would tell my mother such-and-such anyway. After all, I am a rebel! She'd simply reply, "Okay." It was confusing to me as a child because I was always anticipating a huge reaction. Sometimes there was one, and sometimes there was none. So I ask again—are we going to enable others by worrying about their reactions to "protect" their feelings or we going to help them get closer to God...and to us?

Perhaps the best way I've ever summed up my story is with a blog post I wrote in 2016. I titled it "Crazy Love: How to Love the Mentally Ill without Losing Yourself."

> *When I tell people I have a crazy mother a variety of things happen.*
> *The first and most common response is people say, "Who doesn't?"*
> *I generally say, "No, really. My mother is crazy."*
> *And they say, "So is mine."*

Out of curiosity and searching for an empathetic connection, I ask, "What kind of crazy things did your mother do?"

They explain how they couldn't understand their mother's actions or grasp the reasons for her harsh and punitive responses.

For example, a friend shared how much her boys "hated" her when she adopted a portion of a road and had them pick up trash on Saturday mornings. Or how she refused to allow them to have a Nintendo like all the other kids had.

Having a crazy mom is very different than having a mom who is crazy in love with you. I am so glad that many people have moms that are crazy in love with them.

That is not my experience.

When I say I have a crazy mother, I mean mentally ill. Her brain chemistry is different.

A mentally ill mother doesn't adopt a portion of the road and teach her child work ethic and community consciousness when she believes people are trying to run her off the road.

Being able to have a Nintendo isn't a priority when your mother tells you there's no need for you ever to come home. I know most mothers crave for their adult children to come for a visit.

My mother may schedule a visit for me to come over; however, nine times out of ten, she calls at the last minute to say that the thought of me being there is too stressful for her.

<u>Second Response</u> – Defense, Blame, & Invalidation

The second reaction I get is defense, blame, and invalidation.

People defend my mother by saying, "I bet she didn't mean what she said."

And people tend to blame me for how she mothered me. They say things like:

"When that happened, why didn't you tell the neighbors?"

or

"It wasn't that bad. Y'all had money."

For me these statements are the backbone of what is wrong with our society. So many of us perpetuate the cycle of pain and then yell about it when problems continue.

<u>Third Response</u> – Empathy

The third is a beautiful picture of empathy. There are people out there who know what it is like to have a mother who believes people are following her at Harris Teeter or writing "Go Away" in lipstick on her car.

Not that I wish mental illness on anyone, but when I encounter people who struggle with mental illness or know what it is like to love someone who struggles, it is an impenetrable bond.

A true bond doesn't enable victimization; it provides realization and subsequent emotional and spiritual freedom.

For me to heal, I need to see clearly what I have experienced. Then I can receive empathy and support, and, eventually begin to repair.

At some point, God showed me that my mother's story, and her mental illness, no longer had to add pain to my story.

He showed me how to love her without losing myself. God taught me to honor my mother but never to honor harmful behavior.

He showed me purpose, and in that, He re-purposed my life experience into a voice for the suffering.

My mother has never been crazy in love with me.

Surprisingly, I did not spend my childhood thinking I wanted a different mother. Instead, I swam in the cesspool of shame and blame attempting to figure out how I could be more of who she wanted me to be.

As an adult, I had to decide whether I would spend my life trying to change for her or accept the love that was so readily available for me.

No, the love wasn't from her. It was even better. It was from Him. Accepting that she didn't love me the way I needed was step one for me. The second step was knowing who did love me.

God has loved and known me since before conception. He became my focus.

God told me one day, "Stop focusing on the one who hurt you the most, and start focusing on the One who hurt the most for you."

My life changed at that point.

*None of the things my mother did to me changed. My past was not altered. Instead, my **focus shifted**, and I got better.*

*For me, seeking love from a mentally ill mother was similar to pouring water into a bottomless cup. I realized I was standing beside the well of living water with a defective cup, and I **really** was thirsty.*

I had a choice to make.

I realized that my mother was no longer the problem.

*The problem was **my expecting her to do something that history vividly demonstrated was not in her to do**.*

It was time for me to drink from His well instead of the worldly cup of approval.

The most important step in my freedom from our toxic relationship was to surrender approval-seeking behavior. It was scary and uncomfortable. I didn't do this perfectly then, nor do I do it perfectly now.

Every boundary and every new behavior that I feared would make me more motherless than I already was actually created healthy space in our relationship.

In time, compassion replaced codependency and as a daughter of the Almighty Father I became the proud, emotionally free daughter of my mother.

I claimed who I was in Him first, and then I was able to claim her as my mother.

Today, my mother and I talk almost every day. Most of the conversations are fun and resemble normalcy.

There are still some days when she is too ill to understand the intent of my words, and I realize I am speaking to paranoia rather than my mother.

It still hurts my heart but it no longer stops me from a life of love.

I do not want a different mom. I claim her.

I can say with some certainty that she claims me as well.

However, I do not need her to do so because I know the One who created love, loves me.

I can accept my mother and overall those around me because I first accepted who I am in Him. He is crazy in love with me.

AA has a slogan: If nothing changes, nothing changes. Boundaries allow us to navigate our relationships and share with others what we need. Our boundaries fight against shame. They protect us from toxic relationships. They remind us of who we are in Christ and not who others tell us to be. Boundaries shift our focus and help us to gain agreement with God and not with our enemy. If we do nothing in our pain, our pain will remain the same. If we don't set boundaries, our dysfunctional relationships will thrive and we will not feel the full measure of worth God intended us to feel.

There are two significant times in my alcoholism recovery when my eating disorder absolutely took over my life. One of those times is relevant to understanding my story and my ability to have boundaries and a voice. The one I want to share with you took place early in my sobriety. I wrote a list of things I wanted to do for myself, and that action alone caused me to plummet into an abyss of self-hatred.

During my time in this abyss, I went to my parents' house. It was still the same house where I had my first drunk and blackout. At the time of this story, I am sober from alcohol, but I am not emotionally sober. I am not free. Immediately when I arrived at their house, I went for a run. When I returned a little while later, I grabbed some food and took it to "my room." There, I binged and purged. A binge can be two bites of food for some people. For me, at this point, any food I ingested felt like a binge, and I had to get it out of me.

After I was finished, I rode my bike for miles and miles. I came back to my parents' house and hit the repeat button. I ate and purged. Next, I went swimming. You can guess what happened next. After I finished swimming, I binged and purged. Then I left their house.

I drove all the way to South Carolina to see my parents, but all I did was play hide and seek with my pain. Once I was free of my eating disorder, I was able to make sense of my senseless activities that day in my parents' home. One of my most significant emotional needs is to be seen. The wounded child within me wanted them to see my disorder. I desperately wanted my mother to ask if she had caused it, to take ownership in some way.

I was seen that day. My Heavenly Father saw me. I know that now. Not long after that day, He set up a divine appointment and introduced me to a psychotherapist named Connie Burns, and my life changed again.

Connie is the epitome of empathy and compassion. She lived ninety minutes from my home, but I knew I wanted what she had to offer. Every Friday, I traveled to my sessions with her. She nurtured me. She loved me. She challenged me. I assume she did what many good enough mothers do for their children. She also taught me about a form of therapy called P.E.E.R. (Primary Emotional Energy Recovery). It was through her that I learned the founder of P.E.E.R. was John Lee. His work and philosophy helped me understand why the creation of my self-care list evoked such self-hatred and caused me to plummet into that abyss.

Connie gently suggested I read John's book *Growing Yourself Back Up*. My friends, this book resonated with me so much that I tracked John down, called him, and thanked him. It started a lifelong friendship.

I comprehended the fact that I had given my mother all my power. The little girl in me was waiting and longing to be nurtured, but my adult self had to realize this was equivalent to expecting someone without arms to give me a hug. In *Growing Yourself Back Up*, John Lee explains Unahipili. (Yeah, I can't pronounce that for nothing.) Unahipili is the little one in us who remembers everything. We carry all of our past memories within us. Here is one of the hundreds of nuggets of insight from his book: "...feeling small is not a normal part of daily life, and believing that it is destructive. This is one reason why it is imperative for us to understand emotional regression. When we are not conscious of it, it usually brings about damaging behaviors, and inefficient ways of communicating and interacting with others. When we mistake regression for ordinary ways of thinking, speaking, feeling, and acting, we begin living lives of 'quiet desperation' without knowing why."

Through all this life-changing therapy, I was able to identify many toxic beliefs that kept me from living out my true identity. The lies that we don't identify live in our subconscious and become our false identity. I believed the following lies:

If I do enough, I will be good enough.
If I can be the reason you change, I will be worthy.
If I neglect myself enough, you will notice me.
If I hurt enough, you will validate me.
If I play small and let you feel big, you won't leave me.

It is impossible to carry these negative beliefs and not become rageful. I learned during this time that a significant and continuous motivator for my eating disorder was rage. Rage is different than anger. Anger is a God-given emotion while rage is a plethora of emotions suffocating our souls and exploding out as negative behaviors. Every purge was an act of rage. Every time I restricted my food intake, I was acting out my restricted feelings of love. I felt small in importance but carried around a huge amount of disappointment.

I learned from Connie and John that I wasn't meant to live small. Through my eating disorder, I was trying to show how insignificant and unseen I felt in relationship with my mother. When I connected what I learned about emotional regression with God's Word, His message of grace and mercy was absolutely reinforced. God did not send His Son to be crucified and resurrected for me to live small. It was with this determination and sense of belonging to Him that created a foundation for me to be able to later do what God so clearly told me to do – reconcile with my mother.

The new knowledge about emotional regression blended well with what Tracey had taught me about TA (Transactional Analysis). At this point, I was able to get to know my adult self. In my near future, I would also be able to remain in my God-adult self for longer intervals.

Instead of expecting my mother to stop treating me the way she was, I learned I had the power to stop what I was doing. I had to realize I had no power because I did the same things as an adult as that of a powerless little girl. I had to separate the true victim (little girl) from my victim mentality. I chose to divorce the mentality and commit to rescuing the little girl. I stopped neglecting myself and ceased hopelessly yearning for my mother to notice my deep pain and realize she was the cause. To have an adult relationship with her—and more importantly with myself—meant I had to stop having the thoughts and expectations that belonged to an 8-year-old.

---

8 ACTIONS I STOPPED FOR MY 8-YEAR-OLD SELF

- *I stopped minimizing what was happening to me and admitted how much I was affected by it.*
- *I stopped treating myself the same way she treated me. I hated how she treated, me but I had learned to treat myself in the same manner. I could not change her, but I could change how I was interacting with myself.*
- *I decided my own boundaries and limits. If that meant phone calls that lasted for ten minutes or until three insults occurred (whichever came first), then I had to commit to that margin. When I enforced this boundary, I gave myself the message that I was worthy.*
- *I thought it well before I spoke it. Initially, I would say what I wanted to say in my head while staring at my mother or on the phone with her. I knew I wasn't able to say it aloud yet. Doing so made me smile, and in time, I found my voice.*

- *I was willing to be emptied, experience the emptiness (as I was accustomed to the chaos), and then trust I would be full one day. It was imperative for me to admit to myself that the chaos and dysfunction with my mother had become part of my identity. I had to surrender the relationship I thought we should have and the pain of not having that relationship to allow His love to come in and fill me up.*
- *I stopped waiting for an apology. I wanted her to own the past, but I had to realize we would never get to our past unless I buried it. I learned that being stuck in a pattern doesn't allow you to have a past because everything is about the present. You don't get "past" anything. Where there is burial there is resurrection.*
- *I stopped blaming myself for her actions. Blame and responsibility don't know each other. I had to take responsibility for my part and provide her with accountability for what was hers.*
- *I accepted she didn't like me, and I decided that fact didn't mean I didn't have to like myself.*

I have written this before, but it bears repeating: God told me to stop looking to the one who hurt me the most and start looking to the One who hurt the most for me. I wasn't powerless. His Power resides within me. The more I set boundaries, discovered my truth, and uncovered my hidden pain, the more I could see how worldly lies had covered a beautiful, resilient authentically imperfect daughter. And that, my friends, is called recovery.

CHAPTER 17

THE RIGHT PERSON

We are not called to be overwhelmed by our stories.
We are called to be overwhelmed by God's love in our story.

~ KBH

God has a way of pulling everything together at just the right time. As I was working with my friendly ghostwriter to end this tale and plop a big, pink plaid bow on the cover, my mother became sick. My dad had been diagnosed with pneumonia a few weeks earlier. His illness had been so bad that the one who never missed a day of work in his life had missed two weeks. As a matter of fact, his eardrum had burst from his incessant coughing. As soon as he started to feel better, he returned to work. That's just the kind of person he is—even into his seventies.

Then, I watched my mother start to lose her health right behind him. She claimed it was the flu (this was the year of the nastiest flu in recent history), and she tried to convince me she was fine. She told me to leave her alone about a dozen times. However, I could tell she was worsening when I dropped off food one weekend.

After church, my friend and I went to Target to get groceries that I would then take down to my parents' house. I jokingly mentioned to this friend that I would text her later about how my mother complained about the items we picked out. When I arrived, my mother only held onto her stomach and cried. She simply replied, "Thank you." There was no witty remark or complaint about my grocery selections. I returned to my car and knew there was nothing cute to text to my friend. Instead, I texted my running partner: *My mother is dying. Please pray.*

Later, I called my parents' home to check in with them. My mother couldn't hear me through the phone. Her answers to questions started making no sense; she wasn't lucid. I knew the illness—whatever it was—was quickly progressing. Unfortunately, Xenia, in all her agoraphobic splendor, refused with the little might she retained to seek out medical care. Every day, I begged my mother in texts and on phone calls to go to the hospital. "I don't want you to die. Please go to the hospital."

Finally on March 6th at 4:54 a.m., she called me. I didn't wake up until 5:09 a.m. I called her over and over until 5:17 when she finally answered.

As I drove down the interstate to South Carolina like a bullet train, I thought about how my mother couldn't be there for me when I was in the Intensive Care Unit in high school. I recalled the time I was hospitalized in my early thirties for meningitis and never once thought of calling my family.

I knew my father, even though still sick, was in the same house with her, but she chose to call me. She reached out to the daughter she had always rejected. She asked for help from the one not pretty enough. The one not good enough. I had stopped believing all those lies some time ago. All of the recollections and the knowledge of my Savior's love allowed me to smile and feel redeemed. I knew what the enemy had planned for my life no longer bore any weight. It was an honor and a privilege to be the one she called. She called me and I was able to respond because years before, I had accepted that He called me to be repurposed. The significance of the moment was not lost on me. I believe part of the reason she could reach out to me was because I had been calling her every day; perhaps she felt significant and loved.

Isaiah 6:8 declares, "Then I heard the voice of the Lord saying, 'Whom shall I send? And who will go for us?' And I said, 'Here am I. Send me!'" With this one invitation from my mother to help her, my heart and soul felt complete.

When I got to my parents' home I found my dad dressing my mother. This had never, ever happened. I looked in my mom's eyes and saw death. I could barely see her through the blank stare and glazed-over eyes. My years of dissociating as a child came in handy at that moment as I quickly felt nothing but urgency. My daddy followed us to the hospital. As I drove her, I honestly didn't know what to do or say.

Do not be fooled. Xenia was still Xenia. She was sitting next to me whimpering and combing her hair. Yes, she was combing her hair. She is a beautiful woman, and she wanted to do what she could to maintain her beauty and her pride. I took the brush away from her since the movement was clearly causing her pain. I wanted to comfort her, to show her love. Truthfully, I didn't know how so I thought about my dog (really, any dog). Dogs are so easy to love. So, I patted her on the head and kept repeating, "Good puppy."

When we reached the Emergency Department entrance, there was a "redneck" pickup truck in the lane in front of us. I jumped out of my car and ran into the lobby to get some help. "My mom's in the car, and she's dying. I could use some help."

No one moved. Perhaps it was my calm tone despite the meaning of the words I used. The Emergency Department staff just stared at me. From my experience working (and living) in healthcare facilities, I understand that emergencies can be defined differently, and the staff has likely been desensitized to trauma and life-and-death situations. Then someone did move. It was the redneck driver of the redneck truck. He grabbed a wheelchair and started toward my car. The man was trying to help, but I knew what my mother would think. I knew how she would react to his physical appearance, and I couldn't take the risk that she would refuse to get out of my car. So, I gave the poor man *a look*. I hated to have that thought, but I realized it was not mine. It was my mother's bias. I didn't have to carry that shame for her. I let it go, for my mother desperately needed care. What a powerfully restorative experience.

Thankfully, a security guard seized the wheelchair from the man and assisted my mother out of the car and into one of the places she had tried to avoid her whole life—a hospital.

It turned out she had pneumonia that had worsened, and she had become septic. My limited medical experience came in quite handy since my extremely intelligent father, who as you may remember had a burst eardrum from his pneumonia, sat in the corner quietly recovering. My mother wasn't lucid so she could not offer any assistance for her own care. I spent hours in the Emergency Department talking to every medical professional that entered the area. They started antibiotics and searched throughout the hospital (and other local hospitals) for a bed. I was aware of her symptoms and medical history because God had told me years ago to call her every day. I had been the one on the phone with her for years hearing about bowel movements, doctor visits, and the many aging body processes that had caused me to roll my eyes. But He used it all. He knew exactly what He was doing through me and for us many years ago.

, the first hours at the hospital, I couldn't complete
I just expressed to you in this book. I knew I had to stay
on communicating clearly. I thanked God because my relatic
with her centered on my relationship with Him and not on my p
pain. I was close enough to her to understand her medical history
and effectively communicate with the professionals about her signs
and symptoms.

Sitting there among the chaos of the Emergency Department,
my mother turned her head slowly and looked at me as I spoke to
everyone. There were many moments when I could tell it wasn't really
her behind the glazed expression. I decided to braid her hair to pass
the time. The only reason I knew how was because she forced me to
join Girl Scouts where I learned this technique. My braiding skills
made me laugh, and I think that somehow comforted her. In that
Emergency Department, I understood for the first time what Holy
Comforter really meant. She was finally admitted several hours later.

I visited her often in the hospital. Friends in Fort Mill, South
Carolina offered to visit her or help in any way they could. I
respectfully declined (though admittedly, in my head was really
shouting, "NO!"). People with good intentions wanted to decide our
needs and to take care of the situation. This was my Esther moment,
my God-ordained moment. I should have died countless times in my
youth and adolescence. I knew I had been saved for such a time as
this. I was no longer just broken; I was gracefully broken. Gracefully
broken and carefully repaired in order to be part of this redeemed
relationship between mother and daughter.

Broken + Grace = Redeemed.

I had been bringing all my weaknesses to the Lord, and He had
been turning them into something else. No...no one else should—or
could—have been a part of this mother-daughter moment. This was
about the fulfillment of needs. It wasn't about everyone else. It wasn't

.vorite child—my brother. He had moved to New Jersey .nly present through texts. It wasn't about my father. He did .ning he could but knew he needed to get better, too. It wasn't .ut all the people offering to cook food, which would have been a waste of their time since my mother only allowed certain foods in the house. It wasn't about anyone but God, Xenia, and me. He was completely and perfectly restoring what I didn't even think could be improved. She had called me. No one else. This was my time to be there for her in a way she couldn't be for me. Not just a piece of me healed, but many pockets of pain were overtaken with God's grace and mercy over the course of these days.

One night in the hospital, I was arranging her pillows for her when she said she was cold. I asked her if she saw a bright light (Honeycutt humor, folks). She shot me *a look*. My heart relaxed. That look meant she was getting better.

Another night, I was petting her on the head saying, "Good puppy," and she confessed, "I'm ashamed of how I look."

"Mother, you have a lot to be ashamed of. How you look isn't one of them." She flipped me off.

Progress. The way my family speaks to each other probably isn't how your family speaks to each other. Interesting enough, this bizarre wit is what helped me believe she was regaining her SELF—the very self that used to avoid everything and not appreciate others was coming back. The one who caused me confusion was getting better. Now with God as the center of my life, all this gave me so much clarity.

The following visit, my mother's mental illness was in full bloom, exacerbated with the virus and sepsis. She was truly bat-poo crazy. (My ghostwriter cleaned this up. Just saying.) Apparently, the hospital staff was racist and people were out to get her. It was reminiscent of the delusions from my childhood, like when she thought there was a ram in our front yard that had a message for her. Or, like the countless times of her leaving the house and coming back with stories of how people tried to run her off the road.

Upon my arrival, she started sobbing. She truly believed people were trying to hurt her and put dangerous things into her body, and she was afraid. Then she began to direct her onslaught toward me: "You've been a challenge since day one. You were a horrible kid."

The words had no impact. I was in complete agreement with what God says about me—that I am worthy. I am loved. Her words had no power over me because His power is in me. Please don't misunderstand me. I'm human. There are times I do feel her words. On this day, I hurt *for* her. But I didn't become her hurt. I could see it and understand it, but it was hers. Not mine. I did not personalize it or allow it to dictate my sense of my God-self.

When people tell me my mom is not crazy, I do sometimes want to punch them in the throat. Sorry. Not sorry. They weren't there for the ram in the yard. They weren't there when she came home from Southpark Mall (the upscale shopping headquarters in Charlotte, North Carolina) and told everyone that someone had written *No one wants you here. Go back to Fort Mill.* on her car window. They weren't there in the hospital room with us during this illness either. This is my family's reality, and no one should pretend they know more about it than I do. When people tell me I am blessed and should be thankful because she is alive while they lost their mothers, it is very invalidating. When people say, "But she loves you," they are speaking from their experiences and not allowing the conversation or meaning to be about my life experiences.

One night, I just did not want to go to the hospital. It was an hour's drive from my work, and my schedule was booked with patients until 7:00 p.m. Visiting hours ended at 9:00 p.m. I was conflicted. I had talked to my mother on the phone twice that day, and both times she verbally attacked me and then sobbed uncontrollably. I didn't want to make the drive if that was what would continue to happen in person. I texted my BFF (Best Friend Forever), a Physician Assistant, for advice:

Why don't you ask your mom if she wants to see you?

Brilliant.

I called my mom and was thinking of all the times she told me she didn't want me to come see her over the years. *Please let this be one of those times.* I just didn't want to drive down and be lambasted on this particular night. My mother answered the phone, but she couldn't hear me well at all. Her hearing was still depressed as a symptom of the virus in her body. I did, however, clearly hear her say, "Come see me tonight and bring me hair clips." *Good grief.*

"Okay. Okay. I am coming, but I am not bringing you hair clips."

My last patient was tremendously flexible, and we made arrangements for me to be able to talk with her on the phone as I drove to the hospital. I am so thankful I went that night. God had plans—continued plans for the restoration of our relationship. I could have missed it.

The nurse explained that Xenia wouldn't give her blood for the final electrolyte test for discharge purposes. My mother's paranoia was limiting her care. She believed they were stealing her blood, harming her in some way. I can speak medical lingo, so I asked the nurse, "Are you going to discharge her AMA (Against Medical Advice)?"

The nurse said she would have to if my mother refused the labs.

"Do you think she's competent? My father and I will fight her release if she still needs to be here or needs to be cleared for discharge." The nurse looked at me unwaveringly, and I knew I would have to get through to my mother despite her insanity.

I sat on the bed with her. This may sound like a simple act or an easy thing to do. For us, engaging in physical closeness was never a normal behavior. I did the only thing I knew to do. (You guessed it.) I patted her on her pretty head and repeated, "Good puppy!"

I knew I had to connect to her on her level, break through the paranoia, and somehow get her to trust me. I looked at my mother, and I heard the suspicious-sounding internal monologue that had been the customary thoughts and lies from years ago. God had restored our relationship, and over the span of the previous years, I had heard these types of false accusations less and less. But now, in the hospital sitting next to my mother, I suddenly recalled how I used to feel unsafe.

My mother had regressed to her original place of trauma and she was scared. I knew there was no real threat to her; it was a perceived threat from the enemy and her mental illness, but it was real to her. I comforted her from the all the positions I could: that of psychotherapist, of daughter, and most of all, from knowing I am His.

"You have a choice for what you do next. It is your body, and I know you are tired of people probing you. I would feel the same way. You can refuse any further treatment, but if you don't let them take your blood, you're going to get a bill for $200,000. Or, you can give one more vial and pay $0. If you don't cooperate, that means no St. John's (clothing store), no Burberry, and no Neiman Marcus visits. You have primary and secondary insurance. But if you refuse medical treatment, they will discharge you AMA and neither insurance company has to pay. You are one blood test away from going home and keeping money in your pocket or one blood test refusal away from sufficient debt. It is your choice."

My mother looked at me, and she reached up and grabbed my hand. Comfort. Trust. There was a charged flicker of understanding.

Human hands house more than 7,000 nerve endings. They were all firing straight up into my brain. It was so very healing. It was the most connected we had ever been. This electrified connection between mother and daughter may seem commonplace for you and your loved ones. I hope it is. I have no memory of ever holding my mother's hand until that moment. Patting her head, comforting her, bonding with her on a level that required full trust, the physical proximity...it was a sweet experience I never expected I would—or could—have with my mom.

Mom. Not Mother that night. Mom.

While holding my hand, she whispered, "I will pray about it ... and stop calling me puppy."

"That is good enough for me, Mom. Good enough."

Early the next morning, I received a text from my mom stating she allowed the nurse to draw her blood. They checked her electrolytes, and she was released later that day.

On that night, I was the right person. On that night in the hospital room, we were good enough for each other, close enough (physically and emotionally), and able to simultaneously know true worth comes from the One who is truly worthy.

Interestingly, my special visit with her when she held my hand was on her seventh day in the hospital. When she came to see me in the intensive care unit after my fall from the balcony at age fifteen, it was my seventh day in the hospital. I was released on the eighth day, and so was she. Our God is a God of completion.

I celebrated my 47th birthday while my mother was in the hospital. I saw her on March 11th. My father, of course, was there. He gave me a birthday card that contained a serious amount of cash. He also contacted me on my actual birthday and offered me some of his infectious love. My mother? Not so much. She didn't say a word about my birthday. Yes, it is true that she was "doped" up, but this was just like every other year. Somehow now, it was close enough for me.

Without the restoration God had provided and with which I had to be obedient, I don't know what would have happened to my mom during that illness. I don't know who would have been there. I don't know if anyone would have gotten that phone call. There are so many "ifs." I now encourage people to know their own needs and trust people when they express their needs.

It's strange, but now I find myself feeling mad. Well, angry. My mother taught me that only dogs get mad; I wasn't allowed to use that word as a little girl. So to honor her I will tell you that I am angry because one day, my mother is going to die, and now, it will really matter to me. In my past, if she had passed, I would have grieved the mother I had and the mother I didn't have. Through reconciliation and His peace, one day I will grieve the exact mother that I had because for me she is more than good enough.

Yes, the relationship between my mother and me has been messy. We are two different people in every sense. As a little girl, I viewed her as perfect. Consequently, I assumed I was the epitome of imperfection. Our story is of a mother and daughter who could not be more different but through God, found commonality, cleansing, and connection. And that is good enough for me.

When people utter the phrase, "But your mother loves you," they are unintentionally invalidating what God did to restore our relationship. In order for me to have reached the place where I could experience and appreciate her flavor of love, I had to stop minimizing how much her lack of love and her neglect had debilitated me.

If you have someone in your life who is toxic—particularly a parent—please do not misunderstand the true purpose of this book. I put aside my beliefs about who I was within the context of the abuse (and learned who I really was) long before I re-entered my mother's life. I do not believe we are meant to be around people who don't allow us to be our best, most authentic selves. My story has a happy ending, but even if I had not reconciled with my mother, my story would still include a positive outcome. Why? I stopped seeking other people's approval and started living for His. It is difficult, if not impossible, to be abused by a husband, boss, child, sibling, parent, or a friend and remain spiritually cleansed and emotionally regulated. My story isn't your story. It is mine.

I pray that you will take care of yourself. My hope is that you will never believe that someone's deflection of himself or herself is the totality of your Godly reflection. I hope you know that when we accept the right support and participate in internal ownership, the day comes when external lies no longer sound more believable than truth. Then, we trust the Voice within. We are who He says we are. Our worth is as vast as the tomb is empty. We are good through Him. We are enough in Him.

We are good enough.

ABOUT THE AUTHOR

Kim Honeycutt, MSW, LCSW, CCFC, LCAS graduated from Columbia College with a bachelor's degree in psychology and received her master's degree in social work (MSW) from the University of South Carolina. She is a licensed clinical social worker, certified clinical forensic counselor, and licensed clinical addictions specialist. For over twenty years, Kim's psychotherapy practice in Charlotte, North Carolina has helped hundreds of individuals detox from shame and become free of self-destructive behaviors.

Before all the credentials that today reside behind Kim's name, Kim's primary accomplishment was being able to drink a fifth of liquor and still make it to math class. Kim spent over a decade indulging in behaviors such as being arrested, frequenting emergency rooms, being institutionalized, and going to any length to cover her pain. After achieving sobriety and engaging in countless hours of therapy, she found a way to use her pain as a stepping stool. As a result, she implemented numerous creative strategies for releasing shame and today enthusiastically assists others to repair and repurpose their own struggles. Kim's life experiences have afforded her a strong sense of empathy and compassion.

In addition to providing therapy, she has been published in several magazines and has been featured on National Public Radio and "The Debra Kennedy Show." She has spoken at various schools and churches and was honored to be a TEDx Charlotte speaker. Kim is the Founder and President of icuTalks, a mental health speaking ministry in the Charlotte, North Carolina area.

When Kim isn't speaking, providing therapy, or participating in community projects, she is a runner–a very slow runner but a runner nonetheless. Visit www.kimhoneycutt.com and www.icuTalks.com for more information.

Morgan James makes all of our titles available
through the Library for All Charity Organization.

www.LibraryForAll.org

9 781642 791914